THE CREATION OF DANGEROUS
VIOLENT CRIMINALS

THE CREATION OF DANGEROUS VIOLENT CRIMINALS

LONNIE H. ATHENS

R

ROUTLEDGE

London and New York

First published 1989
by Routledge
11 New Fetter Lane, London EC4P 4EE
29 West 35th Street, New York, NY 10001

© 1989 Lonnie H. Athens

Printed and bound in Great Britain by
Biddles Ltd, Guildford and King's Lynn

British Library Cataloguing in Publication Data

Athens, Lonnie H.
  The creation of dangerous violent criminals.
  Includes index.
  1. Criminal psychology. 2. Crime and criminals.
3. Violent crimes--Psychological aspects. I. Title.
  HV6080.A728   1989   364.3'01'9   88-23972

ISBN 0-415-02837-X

Contents

39739

εις Marilyn and Maureen

Preface

I would like to explain why I chose the title, *The Creation of Dangerous Violent Criminals*. I mean this phrase to express how people who commit heinous violent crimes are created. Although I want to avoid giving away my explanation for this problem, I can safely say that it does not closely resemble any of the explanations which existing theories provide. To offer one hint as to the nature of the explanation to be provided, in reading this book one should find that one is undergoing similar thoughts and feelings as the subjects. Thus, the book may be thought of as providing a very crude self test of its own validity for reasons that will become clearer as it is read.

I had originally intended to provide an explanation not only of how people become violent criminals, but also of how they later become non-violent after having earlier been violent. Unfortunately, because I had to rely almost exclusively on out-of-pocket money to perform this study, I ran out of resources before I could complete the entire project as I had originally envisioned it. Besides expanding the scope of the theory, completing the project would probably have resulted in only a few changes in the theory developed; although it might have resulted in significant changes in the policy implications drawn.

This book can be loosely thought of as providing a companion to my earlier book, *Violent Criminal Acts and Actors*. In that book, I primarily provided an explanation of the nature of violent criminal acts and the persons who commit them, whereas in this book, I primarily provide an explanation of how people develop their violent natures in the first place. Thus, while the present analysis may be thought of as providing primarily a genetic explanation in the logical rather than biological sense of the term, my earlier one may be thought of as providing a primarily situational explanation, so that by combining the two, a more complete theory of violent criminality than either analysis can provide alone could be formulated. There are some theoretical differences between the two explanations signaled by my shift in terminology in the present book. My sole objective in the present work was to develop as valid a theory as possible of how dangerous violent criminals are created, without being unduly concerned about its relationship to my prior work.

Lonnie Athens
November 1987
Washington, DC

Acknowledgements

Although the tangible resources available for this project were rather meager, the intangible ones were great and in the long run probably more important than the tangible ones. One of my greatest intangible resources was my late mentor, Herbert Blumer. Just as important as the influence of his teachings and writings on me was the great personal faith which he always expressed in my work. His faith provided the extra confidence I needed to ignore conventional social science dogma about how criminals must be studied and their behavior explained. I confess I always had a great deal of skepticism for conventional social science anyway.

Marilyn O'Rourke Athens was also a great intangible resource. She continually chided me to state the arguments in this book fully that she had heard me make more times than she ever wanted to hear, rather than to moderate them. In fact, she is most responsible for Chapter 11 on policy, which I was reluctant to write and which I almost deleted after I wrote it. Her maxim for my writing this book was analogous to that often given by boxing managers to their fighters: 'Don't leave it in the dressing room' (just talk about it), but 'take it into the ring' (write it in the book). Her deft editorial touch was also invaluable.

Norman Denzin played a similar role, although less directly. His sagacious advice, which I took in the end, was not to try to please conventional criminologists, because in a work such as this I would never be able to please them no matter what I did, so I might as well please myself. Another valuable intangible resource was Heathcote Wales, upon whose peace and tranquility I often abruptly intruded to discuss my latest ideas. Although I seriously doubt whether he gained anything besides numerous headaches from these usually rapid-fire monologues, I was always able to organize my thoughts more successfully as a result of them. Joseph Page, an academic with true literary talent, offered valuable strategic advice, including how to lay out the early chapters of the book. An intangible resource that I cannot fail to mention is my daughter, Maureen who always very effectively, if not always wittingly, played the role of morale booster.

I would also like to thank the shelter for battered women and the various correctional institutions which gave me access to the participants in this study, particularly the juvenile institution which was the source of the majority of the subjects.

I am grateful to Lambros Zaharias, Irene Z. Athens, Erico W. Athens, and Reverend C.N. Dombalis for increasing the odds that I become the author, rather than a possible subject in this book. Finally, one resource this book never lacked was willing and able subjects. I could not have asked for any better subjects than those who participated in this study. Whatever else some of them did or have done since, they fully and freely gave themselves to my study.

1

Dangerous Violent Criminals

CASE 24: MULTIPLE ASSAULT WITH A DEADLY WEAPON

I was cruising around town with two friends of mine, when we suddenly got hit in the rear end by another car. After we stopped off the road, I looked back and saw three guys in the car that hit us. I asked my friends, 'What in the hell were those guys trying to do, kill us?' One of my friends said, 'I don't know what in the fuck they were trying to do. Let's get out and find out.'

When we jumped out, they were already out of their car. The rear bumper of our car was only bent up some, but I was mad because they could have hurt us bad. I said, 'Why in the hell did you run into the back of our car?' They said, 'Why did you stop in the middle of a block so fast?' I said 'Look, you stupid dumb motherfuckers, you ran into us, we didn't run into you.' Then they said, 'We didn't run into you on purpose, you stopped so fast, we couldn't stop in time.' After they said that, I really got pissed off because they didn't act like they were sorry. They didn't seem to give a damn whether they hurt us or not, which got me mad as hell at those stupid motherfuckers. So I said, 'Well, if that's all you dumb motherfuckers got to say about it, let's go on and fight.' They just stood there looking at me dumbfounded, which made my hatred for them explode. I said, 'You're going to be sorry for the day you hit us, you dumb stupid motherfuckers, because now I'm going to kill all three of you.' I decided to get something and really mess them all up bad. I looked in the car and grabbed a heavy steel crowbar. I told my friends, 'Now I'm going to do some real damage to them.' Without saying another word, I started swinging the crowbar and smacked one of the guys hard right in the side of his head. I could feel his skull splatter open when I hit him. He fell to the ground with blood pouring over his face, neck, and shoulders. As I looked at him, he clutched his head and blood ran through his fingers and he screamed, 'Please help me, please help me, my head is bleeding real bad. I'm going to bleed to death.' But I was still mad and could care less whether he lived or died. All I wanted was to get the other two guys before they got away.

Then I turned and quickly hit another one hard across his arm twice while he was still staring at his crying friend who I had hit in the head. After I hit him, he looked at me and squealed, 'Oh my arm, my arm, you broke my arm.' Next I swung and hit the last guy hard in the leg, but I didn't get a chance to hit him solid again. Before I could hit him again and do some real damage to him, he started running with the guy I hit in the arm. I chased those yellow motherfuckers for maybe a half block before I suddenly began worrying about the police getting me. Then I ran back as fast as I could to our car satisfied that I did real damage to two of them. We jumped in the car and drove off fast.

CASE 16: KIDNAPPING AND ATTEMPTED MURDER

James and I got the munchies and were walking to the grocery store to buy some cupcakes. In the parking lot of the store, we saw a fancy camper. I said, 'Check out that camper', and we started looking in its windows. James said, 'That's a bad truck, man.' As we were walking away, an old woman walked by us with a big man pushing her grocery cart. She said, 'Keep away from my truck.' I said 'We were just looking at it.' She said, 'Keep you black asses away from my truck.' After she told us to keep away from her truck, I got mad. After she added the part about our black asses, I got doubly mad and wanted to kill her old stinking ass on the spot. I said, 'Kiss my ass, you old stinking bitch.' The big grocery store man said, 'Get out of here before I call the police.' I said, 'Fuck the police, they're not about anything. I'll kill that old bitch for talking about my black ass.'

About ten minutes later we saw her truck again in a parking lot behind a building. I said to James, 'Look, there's that same damn truck. Now I can get that old bitch.' We ran out to the truck, looked around, and then busted open the back door. I told James, 'When that old bitch comes back, let's take her out some place where I can stomp her ass. I'm going to fuck her up bad.' James only laughed. I was still hot from her referring to our black asses and acting like we were dirt for her to kick around. I wanted to get her old stinking ass bad for saying that to us. I had hate for that old stinking white bitch. James wasn't as mad about her referring to our black asses as I was.

We sat in her camper eating the food she had gotten while we waited for her to come back. I couldn't wait til she saw us. When she came back to the camper, we pulled a knife on her and told her to start driving. She said, 'I'll do anything you want, but please don't hurt me.' As we drove off, she said, 'I'm sorry for what I said to you at the grocery store, please let me go.' We didn't say a word until we told her to pull the camper into a vacant lot we drove past. After she parked the camper, she started crying and slobbering, 'Please don't hurt me, please don't hurt me. I'm sorry, please....' I knew the old stinking bitch was only lying. Seeing her slobber like that only made me madder and hate her even more.

I jumped out of the camper, grabbed her by the shoulders and threw her out of the cab. She landed face first on the dirt. She got up on her hands and knees and started yelling, 'Help, police, help police, help.' I said, 'Shut up you old stinking bitch', and kicked her in the stomach as hard as I could and knocked all the wind out of that old bag. She rolled up in a ball in the mud gasping for her breath, and I kicked her again which straightened her out like a stick. I tried to lift her up by the clothes, but she was so muddy that she slipped out of my hands, so I grabbed her by the hair. James said, 'Would you look at her ugly old face.' After I looked at it, I got so mad, I smacked and backhanded her about twenty times. Then I threw her against the camper and she slumped down on the ground. James opened a can of pop and asked her, 'Do you want some pop?' She said, 'No, I only want you to let me go.' I said, 'I'm not going to let you go, you stinking old bitch. I'm going to kill you.' I grabbed her by the hair again and slammed her head back and forth against the side of the truck until blood started running out from her hair and over her ears. Then I dropped her to the ground, kicked her over into the mudpuddle and left her for dead. We got into her camper and drove off.

As soon as one finishes reading the previous two cases, if not before, one is struck with the thought that these were certainly heinous violent crimes. What may be less obvious is exactly why they merit this pejorative designation. There are two primary reasons why they deserve it. One reason springs from the grievous nature of the violent crimes committed. In the second case presented, the elderly victim nearly died as a result of the horrible injuries she sustained at the hands of her much younger male attacker. In the first case, there were three young male victims rather than only one elderly female. Nevertheless, two of the three victims were very severely injured, with one requiring lengthy hospitalization in order to recover from his wounds. Violent crimes can be considered grievous whenever a major violation of another person's body is committed, whether it is accomplished by the actual infliction of great bodily harm or only the real threat of the infliction of great bodily harm.

The other primary reason why the violent crimes described in the two cases merit the designation of heinous springs from their relative lack of provocation. There are qualitatively distinct degrees of provocation for the commission of violent crimes. Speaking loosely, provocation may range from maximum to moderate, to only minimal, to no provocation whatsoever. Maximum provocation may be said to occur only when the victim's actions place the subsequent attacker's physical safety in imminent danger. In this case, the perpetrator may sometimes later successfully claim that his or her violent action was legally permissible on grounds of self-defense and thereby not a crime. Moderate provocation may be said to occur when victims purposely and cruelly antagonize their subsequent attackers to the point of tormenting them. Although violent crimes which are moderately provoked are not potentially justifiable as are those which are maximally provoked, they are at least somewhat understandable to most people. Minimal provocation may be said to occur when the victims provoke their subsequent attacker, but their provocatory actions fall somewhat short of those just described. For violent crimes to be heinous, there must have been only minimal or less than minimal provocation for their commission.

In neither of the cases presented did the level of provocation exceed the minimal level, although it did vary somewhat between the cases. In the second case presented, the victim's conduct was the more provocative, since she intentionally provoked her subsequent attacker by directly insulting him, but he was in no sense tormented by her. In the first case, the victims' conduct was less provocative, since they unintentionally provoked their subsequent attacker through colliding with the car in which he was a passenger and then failing to offer a proper apology quickly enough. Although the level of provocation in each case differed, it was either minimal or less than minimal in both of them.

Heinous violent crimes, therefore, are those in which the provocation is grossly disproportional to the injuries inflicted upon the victim, so that these are the violent crimes in which people are severely injured or killed with little or no apparent provocation. Most people dread becoming the victim of a heinous violent crime more than any other crime because they fear that without any real provocation on their part, someone could gravely harm them. People justifiably fear that merely by being at the wrong place at the wrong time and by saying and doing the wrong thing or not saying and doing the right thing to the wrong person, they or someone they care about could be seriously injured, maimed, or killed. The likelihood of this happening in our present society is not so remote as to make this a groundless or needless worry for any individual, including those most heavily shielded from the vagaries of social life.

Criminals who commit heinous violent crimes are the most *dangerous violent criminals* in our society, with perhaps the lone exception of certain while collar criminals whose actions jeopardize the health or safety of large numbers of people. Although the term 'dangerous violent criminal' may, at best, seem to be needlessly redundant, it is, in fact, an appropriate way to designate those violent criminals who commit heinous violent crimes. Contrary to the belief of most lay people and criminologists alike, not all violent criminals are equally violent: some are much more violent than others. Those select few violent criminals who will commit grievous violent acts with the least amount of provocation are the most violent ones. That explains why the term 'dangerous violent criminal' is not a redundancy, but an apt designation.

The basic question which the occurrence of heinous violent crimes ultimately raises is: *How* does a human being in our supposedly highly civilized society become the type of person who would commit these violent crimes without any apparent moral qualms or reservations? Or to put it more simply, what makes people become dangerous violent criminals? In this book, I hope to provide a fuller and deeper answer to this troubling question than has been provided before. The chapters that follow should make the process through which dangerous violent criminals are created less dark and mysterious and much more understandable. Unfortunately, the elucidation of the process behind the creation of dangerous violent criminals is not without its drawbacks. Most people's feelings toward dangerous violent criminals are probably morally unambiguous. They have outright hostility towards any violent criminals plaguing their communities and want these criminals swiftly caught and severely punished for burdening them with anxiety and fear over their own and their families' personal safety.

However, people will discover through reading this book that they have had a shortsighted and simplistic view of this very serious problem. When they now look at a dangerous violent criminal, they see only the finished product of a lengthy and at points tortuous developmental process which most definitely ends, but which did not start, with a malevolent human being. A reading of this book will afford a much longer and more complex view of the dangerous violent criminal. When people look at a dangerous violent criminal at the beginning of his developmental process rather than at the very end of it, they will see, perhaps unexpectedly, that the dangerous violent criminal began as a relatively benign human being for whom they would probably have more sympathy than antipathy. Perhaps more importantly, people will conclude that the creation of dangerous violent criminals is largely preventable, as is much of the human carnage which follows in the wake of their birth. Therefore, if society fails to take any significant steps to stop the process behind the creation of dangerous violent criminals, it tacitly becomes an accomplice in creating them. Thus, as a result of this drastic change from a nearsighted and simplistic to a farsighted and complex view of dangerous violent criminals, a real sense of moral ambiguity over this problem is generated which may prove quite distressing.

2

The Key to the Creation of Dangerous Violent Criminals

What is the key to discovering how dangerous violent criminals are created? Perhaps the best way to find the answer to this question is to look at the keys which have already been used to try to unlock the mystery behind their creation. Since different theories offer explanations of phenomena in terms of particular factors or processes to the exclusion of other factors or processes, they may be thought of as providing the keys to the mysteries of the creation of phenomena, whether the phenomenon under consideration be some dreaded disease or dangerous violent criminals. Thus, possible keys to the creation of dangerous violent criminals may be found in the major existing theories which purport to explain it.

The extant theories of how people become dangerous violent criminals can be placed into one of two broad categories: *social environmental* and *bio-physiological*. This classification of theories does not rest upon the presumption that some of the theories exclusively explain becoming a dangerous violent criminal in terms of bio-physiological factors or processes, whereas others explain it exclusively in terms of social environmental factors. Rather, this classification rests only upon the presumption that in all theories, one kind of factor is invariably emphasized to a greater degree than the other. Bio-physiological theories merely place more importance upon bio-physiological factors than upon social environmental ones, whereas social environmental theories place more importance upon social environmental factors than bio-physiological ones. Thus, the present classification of theories into these two categories is based upon their relative, not absolute, emphasis upon one kind of factor or process versus the other. Since all present theories of violent criminality emphasize one kind of factor or process more than the other, there is no theory which cannot easily be placed into one category or the other. In fact, it can be safely stated that virtually all existing theories emphasize one kind of factor or process *significantly* more than the other. Thus, the present classification of theories of violent criminality accurately reflects their current state of development.

Sarnoff Mednick developed what can perhaps be considered the quintessential bio-physiological theory of the creation of dangerous violent criminals from his study of the indices of the autonomic nervous system activities, such as the galvanic skin response (GSR) of criminals and delinquents.[1] Mednick believes that punishment is the most practical and efficient means which society has at its disposal for the moral training of children, and he developed his theory around the notion that children become dangerous violent criminals because of their failure to learn from punishment. Mednick's assumptions are that: the way in which the autonomic nervous system operates in a particular child is largely inherited from his parents; the autonomic nervous system largely regulates the emotion of fear; and the arousal and dissipation of fear, in turn, controls whether or not children can learn from punishment.

Given the importance of the first two assumptions in this theory, a few brief and admittedly oversimplified remarks about the autonomic nervous system are appropriate here. The autonomic nervous system has traditionally been conceived of as consisting of two sub-systems: the sympathetic and the parasympathetic nervous systems. The sympathetic nervous system, which only fully comes into play when the body becomes emotionally aroused, innervates physiological processes such as the heart rate and sweating, the latter of which the GSR is designed to measure. The parasympathetic nervous system, which comes more fully into play when the body is at rest, innervates physiological processes such as digestion. Thus, it appears that Mednick's theory is most directly based upon the operation of the sympathetic sub-system of the autonomic nervous system.

Mednick describes the causal dynamics at work in those who do *not* become a dangerous violent criminal in terms of his four often-cited points:

(1) Child A contemplates aggressive action.
(2) Because of previous punishment or the threat of punishment he suffers fear.

(3) Because of fear he inhibits the aggressive response.

(4) Because he no longer entertains the aggressive impulse, the fear will begin to dissipate, to be reduced.[2]

Mednick later adds a critical fifth point: 'The reduction of fear (which immediately follows the inhibition of the aggression)...act[s] as a reinforcement for this *inhibition* and will result in learning the inhibition of aggression.'[3] (emphasis in original) Mednick underscores the importance of this last point, claiming that 'fear reduction' is the most powerful inducer of learning now known to humankind.

If Mednick's five points were restated in terms of how children *do* become dangerous violent criminals, rather than in terms of how they do *not* become dangerous violent criminals, his theory could be much better understood. I have provided such a restatement below. It should be borne in mind while reading these restated points that only the bare minimum of modifications, which are indicated by italics, were made to his original statement of them.

(1) Child A contemplates aggressive action.

(2) Because of previous punishment or the threat of punishment, he suffers *a relatively diminished amount of fear.*

(3) Because of his *lessened* fear, he does *not* inhibit the aggressive response.

(4) Because he *continues* to entertain the aggressive impulse, the fear *does not quickly* begin to dissipate, to be reduced.

(5) The reduction of fear (which immediately follows the inhibition of the aggression) *does not, thereby*, act as a reinforcement for this inhibition and result in learning inhibition of aggression.

It should be pointed out that Mednick fully acknowledges that punishment of the aggressive action of children is done by 'censuring agents' such as their parents, older siblings, and peers, so that his theory cannot be said to totally ignore social environmental factors. Be that as it may, it is the insufficient arousal of fear from past episodes of punishment for aggressive actions, coupled with the insufficient dissipation of fear in the light of present aggressive impulses, which prevents children from learning to inhibit their impulse to aggress upon others. These two insufficiencies do not stem at all from the faulty administration of punishment on the part of censuring agents, but stems entirely from the faulty operation of the children's autonomic nervous system, or more precisely, sympathetic nervous system which is largely inherited.

Although this theory is very intriguing, it raises some important questions which Mednick has not yet answered. If people become dangerous violent criminals because of their failure to learn from punishment to inhibit their aggressive impulses, then how can one explain why these aggressive impulses so seldom become expressed in violent criminal acts? Obviously, dangerous violent criminals are not continuously committing violent crimes. Second, what is to say that the faulty operation of the sympathetic nervous system which is at the root of this learning disability is not just as much a product of the social environment as it is of the genes? It may be wise to consider here an argument which the anthropologist Ashley Montague has convincingly made:

> We suggest that just as certain areas of the brain are organized by experience to function in the service of speech, so certain specific areas of the brain can be organized to function in the service of aggressive behavior....But that just as speech is not present in the so-called speech areas until it is organized into them, so in man aggression is not present in the so-called aggression areas until it has been organized into circuits by certain kinds of frustrating and related experiences.[4]

In short, Mednick makes the operation of the sympathetic nervous system by far the most important factor in his explanation, and thereby it can legitimately be placed under the category of a bio-physiological theory.

Turning now to social environmental theories, the persons who together developed the quintessential social environmental theory of the creation of dangerous violent criminals are undoubtedly Marvin Wolfgang and Franco Ferracuti.[5] They developed the theory primarily from their study of the differential rates of violent crime, especially criminal homicide, among different social categories of people. They were particularly struck by the almost universally higher incidence of these crimes being committed by males, young adults, non-whites, and members of the lower social class. This lead them to theorize that 'subcultures of violence' exist in societies. A subculture of violence is a system of norms, which prescribes using violent action and proscribes using non-violent action to settle disputes, and values, which place a premium upon taking the latter as opposed to the former course of action. Thus, for

Wolfgang and Ferracuti, a subculture of violence is different from the larger 'dominant' culture, not in terms of its entire system of norms and values, but only in terms of the part related to violence. Nevertheless, the internalization of violent values and norms by members of this subculture directly manifests itself in their attitudes and personality characteristics – attitudes and personality characteristics which sharply distinguish them from members of the dominant culture.

Wolfgang and Ferracuti set out their theory in a set of what they call 'corollary propositions' stated below:

(1) No subculture can be totally different from or totally in conflict with the society in which it is part.

(2) To establish the existence of a subculture of violence does not require that the actors sharing in these basic value elements should express violence in all situations.

(3) The potential resort or willingness to resort to violence in a variety of situations emphasizes the penetrating and diffusive character of this culture theme.

(4) The subcultural ethos of violence may be shared by all ages in a subsociety, but this ethos is most prominent in a limited age group, ranging from late adolescence to middle age.

(5) The counter-norm is non-violence.

(6) The development of favorable attitudes toward, and the use of, violence in a subculture usually involve learned behavior and a process of differential learning association, or identification.

(7) The use of violence in a subculture is not necessarily viewed as illicit conduct and the users therefore do not have to deal with feelings of guilt about their aggression.[6]

Unfortunately, these corollary propositions raise some important questions which the theory does not answer. First, precisely how do the violent norms, values, attitudes, and unspecified personality characteristics alluded to in this theory combine together in the aforementioned variety of situations, but not in all situations, to produce violent criminal acts? Second, and much more importantly for our present concerns, exactly how are the violent values and norms, whose internalization presumably produces the violent attitudes and unspecified personality characteristics, acquired through 'a process of differential learning, association, or identification'?

Neither one of these two fundamental questions is ever clearly answered, either in the above quoted corollary propositions or anywhere else in Wolfgang and Ferracuti's lengthy and often repeated expositions of their highly celebrated theory. One cannot explain this failure carefully to work out the answers to these fundamental questions in terms of their haste in formulating a theory which combined a variety of different ideas since their theory has now been in existence for almost thirty years.[7]

Be this as it may, there are still conclusions which can be drawn with certainty about this theory. The notion of violent subculture does definitely form a causal complex in which violent values, norms, and attitudes, as well as distinctive personality traits play the most crucial parts so that the creation of dangerous violent criminals would definitely be explained in precisely these terms. These violent values, norms, as well as the unspecified personality traits and attitudes produced from them, are obviously conceived as a social environmental acquisition in which bio-physiological factors play little, if any part. If there can be any doubt about this last assertion, the following statement of Wolfgang and Ferracuti should completely dispel it: 'We are lead back to the *external social environment* as the area where the *causative key* to aggression must at present be found'.[8] (emphasis added) Thus, the 'subculture of violence' theory may represent one of the purest instances of a social environmental theory which explains, even if only sketchily, the creation of dangerous violent criminals.

WHY PRESENT THEORIES FAIL TO PROVIDE THE KEY TO THE CREATION OF DANGEROUS VIOLENT CRIMINALS

In the introduction to what may be the most comprehensive review ever undertaken of the part played by bio-physiological factors in criminal behavior, Salem Shah and Loren Roth, the former a renowned forensic psychologist and the latter an equally renowned forensic psychiatrist, state:

Modern geneticists have pointed out that a nature–nurture dichotomy is clearly untenable, incorrect, and meaningless. The subject has to be discussed in terms of the *continuous* and *complex* interactions between an organism and its environment, and the *relevant contributions* of *both sets of variables* in determining the behavior of the organism.[9] (emphases added)

No quarrel whatsoever can be raised here with the assertion that the nature–nurture dichotomy is untenable or that there is a continuous and complex interaction between an organism and its environment. However, a serious quarrel can be raised with the assertion that the relative contributions of the organic body and environment can somehow be ascertained, because it contains an insoluble paradox. If the interaction between an organism and its environment is 'continuous' and 'complex', then how can one ever expect to ascertain the relative contribution of each one to a person becoming a dangerous violent criminal? Of course, the answer is that one cannot.

In their book *Not in Our Genes*, Lewontin, Rose and Kamin drew a similar conclusion about behavior in general, substituting their terms of 'cultural determinism' and 'biological determinism' for my terms of social environmental and bio-physiological theories:

> Extreme cultural determinism is as absurd as its biological bedfellow. Of course, neither biological nor cultural determinists ever wish *entirely* to exclude the significance of the other.... Both sides, however, seem to share in a type of arithmetical fallacy which argues that causes of events in the life of an organism can be partitioned out into a biological proportion and a cultural proportion, so that biology and culture together add up to 100 percent.[10] (emphasis in original)

Moreover, in remarks they make a few short pages after their statements quoted earlier, Shah and Roth show that they completely agree with Lewontin and his associates' argument. Nevertheless, they remain oblivious to the serious contradiction present in their thinking:

> Within the conceptual framework outlined above we cannot, of course, *separate* or *parcel out* the biological from the various social and environmental factors. Indeed, such dichotomous thinking, whether it be 'tilted' towards social and environmental or toward biological variables, *makes little conceptual, logical, or practical sense*. Rather, tendencies toward the dichotomous modes of thinking would serve simply to *limit, obstruct,* and *hinder* a broad, multidisciplinary approach to understanding human behavior in its *natural complexities.*[11] (emphases added)

The statements of Shah and Roth ironically undercut dramatically the value of their later extensive review of the contribution of bio-physiological factors to criminal behavior; but much more important than this, it provides the basis for a devastating critique of *all* bio-physiological or social environmental theories of criminal behavior. Their remarks, together with those of Lewontin and his associates, make abundantly clear that any theory which rests upon the absurd assumption that the causes of human conduct can somehow be arbitrarily divided into bio-physiological and social environmental factors transmogrifies reality and is false on its face.

The implications of the fallacy of constructing dualistic theories may be more far reaching than is immediately realized. It means that the now popularly accepted great theoretical advance of constructing theories of criminality in which both bio-physiological and social environmental factors rather than only one or the other set of factors are incorporated, as the one contained in Wilson and Herrnstein's widely acclaimed book, *Crime and Human Nature*, is completely illusory. Two-sided theories that incorporate both bio-physiological and social environmental factors are no less dualistic than one-sided ones that only incorporate one or the other kind of factor, since both equally operate upon the mistaken presumption that the factors which bring about criminality spring from one of two separate sources – the organic body or the social environment.

A perfect example of this new, more sophisticated form of dualistic reasoning is provided in Mednick's preface to the book, *Biosocial Bases of Criminal Behavior*:

> It is curious that in order to see the action of social forces with more precision we must first account for the variance attributable to genetic and physiological factors. In order to better understand the operation of biological factors, we must first control social variables. We hope this volume can serve to illustrate this method of analysis of sociobiological interplay.[12]

In conclusion, the real key to discovering how people become dangerous violent criminals is to find some way to develop a theory from studying them which does not split in two the bio-physiological and social environmental sources of their violence. Put more positively, the key lies in figuring out some way to develop a theory which *integrates* rather than *segregates* the effects of social environmental and bio-physiological factors. As will be recalled, Shah and Roth's recommendation in this regard was that a 'broad multidisciplinary approach' be taken as a means of resolving this problem. Unfortunately, their proposed solution could do much more harm than good, because it would ultimately lead only to the social environment and human body being carved up into finer and finer separate pieces. With each new scientist from a different field added to the study of the problem, more likely than not only a new division of human conduct corresponding to each one's field of speciality would be created, so that the solution could be pushed infinitely farther away instead of being brought closer at hand. Thus, the solution may lie elsewhere than merely taking a multidisciplinary approach, which has been for some time now the standard nostrum that is prescribed whenever some new stubborn problem arises which blocks progress in the study of human conduct.

From my point of view, the solution to the problem of dualism lies not in taking a multidisciplinary approach which would very likely only compound the problem, but rather in taking a *holistic* approach which could eliminate this problem altogether. If a holistic approach were taken, violent criminals could be studied in a way which does not wrench their organic bodies apart from their social environments, thereby making it possible for the first time to construct a non-dualistic theory of their creation. Thus, the formidable demand that a holistic approach would have to meet is the provision of a bridging concept or some over-arching idea that would fuse together the study of the bodies of criminals with the study of their social environments. Both multidisciplinary and conventional approaches alike keep these torn asunder.

The rather commonplace notion of *social experience* would meet this demand, if properly conceived. As John Dewey pointed out long ago in *Experience and Nature*, a social experience emerges from the special interaction that takes place between a human organism and his social environment during the process of living. This interaction takes the form of human beings *acting* toward one another. What makes it special is that it generates both thoughts and emotions. 'The thing essential to bear in mind', Dewey emphasizes, 'is that living as an empirical affair is not something which goes on below the skin-surface of the organism: it is always an *inclusive* affair involving *connection, interaction* of what is within the organic body and what lies outside in space and time and with higher organisms far outside.'[13] (emphases added) Environment-less social experiences are as impossible to have as body-less ones: just as there are no social experiences without social environments, there are no social experiences without bodies. It should be noted here that the *'connection'* to which Dewey refers between the organic body and the social environment, which incidentally includes thought and emotion, cannot be severed at any point. Thus, during social experiences, the human organism and the social environment are united into an *indivisible* whole. As long as social experience is made the initial starting and returning point for the development of theories of the creation of dangerous violent criminals, then their organic bodies are not chopped apart from their social environments.

It is axiomatic by both their very logic and design that bio-physiological and social environmental theories do not make social experience the basic datum from which they begin and end. This can easily be illustrated with the theories of each respective type reviewed earlier. As will be recalled, Mednick developed his bio-physiological theory principally from his study of patterns in the indices of autonomic nervous system activity, primarily the GSRs of criminals and delinquents. He then suddenly ends with an explanation formulated in terms of criminals' reputed failure to learn from punishment to inhibit their aggressive impulses. Similarly, Wolfgang and Ferracuti developed their social environmental theory principally from their study of the incidence of violent offenders among different social categories of people. Then they suddenly end with an explanation formulated in terms of violent offenders' surmised learning of violent values, norms, and attitudes and development of distinctive personality traits. Thus, nowhere in the empirical findings from which either of these two respected theories were originally formulated or later tested were the social experiences of violent criminals directly taken into account. This failure to study social experiences explains why these theories are cast in such highly mechanistic and unrealistic terms that often strain the credulity of laypeople, even if they do not strain the credulity of most professional criminologists.[14]

As will be recalled, the question with which I opened this chapter was: 'What is the key to discovering how dangerous violent criminals are created?' The answer to this question should now be readily apparent. The key to this discovery will not come through developing theories from studying the social environments of dangerous violent criminals, nor from studying their bio-physiological make-ups. The key will also not come through the study of their social environments in conjunction with their bio-physiological make-ups, as some have done under the erroneous belief that this constituted a major theoretical breakthrough. Instead, the key to the discovery of the creation of dangerous violent criminals lies in developing theories from the careful study of their *social experiences*.

3

The Research Rationale
and Strategy

The ultimate goal behind my research effort was to develop a new theory for explaining the creation of dangerous violent criminals from their intensive study. The achievement of this goal required that I discover how violent criminals are created within some reasonable degree of completeness, fully realizing that no one study or even an entire program of studies could ever yield the complete answer to this difficult question. My study was purposely guided by only a few simple assumptions in order to facilitate the discovery process as much as possible. It only stands to reason that the more assumptions that one makes and the more complicated those assumptions are, the greater likelihood of confirming what is already known or believed and the less likelihood of discovering anything new. From this point of view, the fewer assumptions and attendant preconceptions, the better, since the door is left open for original observations and discoveries.

One critical assumption upon which I operated was that people are what they are as a result of the social experiences that they have undergone in their lives. Thomas Wolfe once said about the characters in his acclaimed novel, *Look Homeward, Angel*, 'Each moment of their lives was conditioned not only by what they experienced in that moment, but by all that they experienced up to that moment,'[1] Although eloquently stated, Wolfe's observation is imprecise. People undergo an almost endless stream of social experiences over their waking lives, but most of them are trivial rather than truly significant in nature. Trivial social experiences have little impact beyond the few moments, minutes, hours, or even days in which they transpired and are forgotten almost as soon as they are undergone. In sharp contrast, significant social experiences are consequential and unforgettable. They have a lasting impact upon people's lives and are remembered weeks, months, and years after the experience was undergone. Significant social experiences leave a permanent mark upon people regardless of their wishes. The social experiences which make people dangerous violent criminals are the significant experiences rather than the trivial ones in their lives.

Criminologists do not, however, study violent criminals' social experiences, either the significant or trivial ones. Instead, some study factors which play upon violent criminals from inside their bodies, such as chromosomes, hormones, or brain waves, either alone or together with those which play upon them from outside their bodies in their social environments, such as subcultures or social stratification. Others study factors which play upon violent criminals from inside their minds, such as psychopathy or sociopathy, either alone or together with one or both of the two prior factors. As a result, the sources of criminal conduct are falsely dichotomized into the separate parts of organic body and social environment, or worse still, falsely trichotomized with the addition of still another separate part – the mind. This trichotomy is worse than the dichotomy because it only further exacerbates the same pernicious problems with the dichotomy uncovered in the previous chapter.

A thorough answer to the question of why criminologists fail to study violent criminals' social experiences would take us too far astray here. Perhaps the single most important reason for this paradoxical development stems from their need to make their studies appear impressive. Most criminologists believe that to be most impressive, they must use mathematics and perform statistical analyses, the more complex the better.[2] But before complex statistical analyses can be performed, social experiences must first be chopped up and shrunken down into 'variables', or discrete entities which easily translate into numbers. As Herbert Blumer has forcibly argued in his book, *Symbolic Interactionism*, however, when social experiences are reduced to numbers, the appearance of precision is almost always gained, but at the unacceptable expense of sacrificing the very heart of the meaning of the social experiences studied.[3] As a consequence of this notorious practice, the basic *integrity* of social experiences is routinely violated in order to force them into variables which arbitrarily split the sources of criminal conduct into two or even three separate spheres – the organic body, the mind, and the social environment.

There is another closely related reason for ignoring the

19

significant social experiences of violent criminals on the part of criminologists. In order to excavate violent criminals' significant life experiences, rapport with them must first be established and then maintained. True rapport is achieved only when communication between two people has reached the point where events in each of their respective lives can be accurately communicated to each other, even if the events are unsavory. The only way in which one can hope to establish such rapport is through prolonged close and intimate contact with the people with whom it is desired. The fact is that the social scientists who have done most of the research on violent criminals are academics. There is certainly nothing in the backgrounds of most of them, either prior to or after coming to the university, that prepares them to achieve rapport with violent criminals. On the contrary, most academics find the average violent criminal so alien and repugnant that they do not want to have any face-to- face contact whatsoever, much less to establish rapport with them. Moreover, academics often cast aspersions upon those researchers who can establish rapport with such persons. Although anyone can understand the desire of academics, like other people, not to have close contact with violent criminals, it is not understandable for those who hold themselves out as experts on this problem.

The usual rebuttal of academic experts on violent crime to the charge that they have little first-hand knowledge of their subject of expertise is that one need not actually *have* heart trouble or some other terrible disease to discover a cure for it. Of course a researcher does not need to have a heart disease in order to discover its nature and cure, but he must at least *see, touch, smell, and examine* actual diseased hearts if he ever hopes to know anything about them. How can one ever expect to get to the bottom of a problem when one scrupulously avoids all direct contact with it? Thus, although one need not *be* a violent criminal to discover the cause of others becoming violent criminals, it is only a matter of common sense that extensive direct contact with violent criminals is absolutely essential if one expects ever to achieve this goal.[4]

A second closely related and equally critical assumption upon which this study operated was that the significant experiences which make people dangerous violent criminals do not occur all at once in their lives, but occur gradually over time. Since later social experiences often build upon earlier experiences, they must form some sort of developmental process with discernable stages.

However, this developmental process is probably not preordained. The earlier stages might make the later stages possible, but *not inevitable*. In other words, it may be that many more people start upon the process than finish it. They could complete some of the earlier stages in the developmental process without ever entering later stages.

The stages in this process can be pictured as a series of chambers, each having two closed doors – one marked 'entrance' and the other marked 'exit'. In order to get to the last chamber, one must first pass through each one of the earlier chambers. One could, however, never reach the last chamber, but could either stay locked in one of the earlier chambers or escape through one of the doors marked exit and leave the edifice altogether.

In this study, I operated upon the third critical assumption that it is far better to study fifty people in depth than to study 5,000 people superficially. Although this assumption is not widely shared among social scientists today, it is shared by some of those in such widely diverse fields as zoology and literature. In *The Art of Scientific Investigation*, W.I. Beveridge, a former professor of animal pathology at Cambridge, has remarked that 'more discoveries have arisen from intense observation of very limited material than from statistics applied to large groups'.[5] In *The Story of a Novel*, Thomas Wolfe made the same point, but in more dramatic terms:

> it is a great deal more important to have known one hundred living men and women in New York, to have understood their lives, to have got somehow at the root and source from which their natures came than to have seen or passed or talked with 7,000,000 people upon the city streets.[6]

Discovering the significant social experiences which a small number of people have undergone over their lives is a much more difficult task than it may appear. Human social experiences can provide a murky and nebulous domain through which one can quickly and easily lose one's way. The key to performing this undertaking successfully is an effective strategy. A strategy need not be overly complicated in order for it to be effective. The strategy which I used to try to discover the experiential process through which dangerous violent criminals are created was a relatively simple one based upon common sense. My common sense strategy, unfortunately, turned out to be more difficult in actual practice than it looks in principle. The social experiences being sought, of course, had to be common to dangerous violent criminals or those on the path to becoming them, but not common to people who were not violent criminals or headed in that direction. Thus, not just any social experiences, even significant ones, shared among dangerous and incipient dangerous violent criminals would suffice. Instead, the experiences had to be the *relatively unique, shared* experiences of dangerous and incipient dangerous violent criminals – the significant life experiences which they shared, but which other people did not share with them.

In applying this common sense strategy, I initially concentrated my efforts on discovering the common significant social experiences of confirmed violent and incipient violent serious criminals. The past significant social experiences of two different groups of violent offenders were examined for this purpose: veterans and novices. The veteran group of seasoned violent offenders was composed of eight male adult offenders who were serving a current sentence in a correctional institution for a serious violent crime and who, in addition, had been previously convicted of at least two prior violent crimes. In contrast, the novice group of unseasoned violent offenders was composed of thirty young adult male and female offenders whose ages ranged from early to late teens and who were serving a sentence in a correctional institution for a serious violent crime. In addition, they all candidly admitted to me that they had committed previous violent criminal acts for which they were able to escape conviction or even arrest.

The assumption upon which I selected these two groups was that the unseasoned violent offenders could provide better and more detailed information on the early stages of the experiential process which makes people dangerous violent criminals, while the seasoned violent offenders could provide better and more detailed information on the later stages and, hopefully, the experiential process as a whole. I also presumed that the veterans would provide the needed insurance that the entire experiential process would be captured and identified, since they were much more likely to have completed the entire process than were the novices.

As it turned out, this assumption was almost totally wrong. Most of the novices had completed the experiential process I ultimately discovered, so that they could provide better and more detailed information in most cases on both the early *and* later stages. Of course, the reason for this was that most of the significant social experiences that comprised the stages usually had more recently happened to the novices than to the veterans. Nevertheless, the veteran group proved invaluable to the analysis, since they provided a synoptic, altogether more cryptic, view of the entire experiential process which quickly alerted me to profitable avenues to explore later with the novice group.

I ascertained the significant social experiences which the seasoned and unseasoned violent offenders had undergone over their lives through privately conducted, in-depth interviews. The interviews usually lasted between seven and nine hours and were divided up into two or three separate sessions, with each session lasting for between two and three hours. It should be stressed that during the interviews, the subjects described the experiences which they, rather than I, deemed significant for their lives and the approximate time in their lives when they had undergone these experiences.

Of course, ideally it would have been preferable to have observed the offenders actually undergoing these social experiences, rather than only interviewing them later about those experiences. Nevertheless, observing people can never obviate the need for conducting interviews with them, because the cognitions and emotions which are embedded in human social experiences can never be fully ascertained purely by observation. A researcher must always ask people about what they felt and thought when they underwent a social experience to ensure that he does not form a bad misconception about these matters. As my analysis will reveal, it would have been virtually impossible, practically speaking, to have observed most of the social experiences which were ultimately discovered to lead people to become dangerous violent criminals. Thus, interviewing turned out to be the only feasible means by which the necessary information could have been gleaned from the offenders.[7]

I analyzed the descriptions that the offenders presented to me during the interviews of their social experiences by the deceivingly simple, but time proven method of constant comparison. More precisely, I continuously compared the offenders' descriptions of their different social experiences against one another to try to isolate the nature of the social experiences which they had commonly undergone and the sequence in which they had undergone them. As a result of making these comparisons for what seemed like an endless time, I developed various provisional experiential processes and their constituent stages. Then I carefully compared these provisional experiential processes against the sequence of significant social experiences undergone by each violent offender, until I finally struck upon the process which seemed to work for all the offenders, the seasoned and unseasoned alike.

After this experiential process – or at least what at the time I thought it to be – was identified, the problem which then arose was that of determining whether or not the experiences comprising the stages in this process were really unique to dangerous and dangerous incipient violent criminals. My fear was that I might have expended a good deal of time and effort only to have discovered social experiences which, although significant to these subjects, were in no way unique to them. In order to avoid this serious pitfall, the significant social experiences of two other groups of persons were subsequently examined in the same manner as those of the veteran and novice violent groups. I conducted private, in-depth interviews with these people to obtain information on their significant social experiences. Then I placed their experiences in sequential order and subjected them to constant comparison.

The first kind of person whose past significant social experiences I examined for this purpose were non-violent criminal males. This group was made up of half a dozen young adult males who had no known arrests for violent crimes and had not reported to me ever committing any serious violent acts for which they had escaped arrest, although they had committed non-violent criminal ones. I chose young adult males instead of older ones because the younger novice violent offenders had earlier proven to be more suitable subjects than the older veterans. I found that some of the members of this new group of subjects had, in fact, undergone some of the social experiences similar to those comprising the early stages of the provisional experiential process earlier identified. Consequently, to my dismay, I had to renew once more the search for the unique social experiences of dangerous violent criminals and drastically to revise the provisional experiential process several times.

Once the new experiential process was developed, I made a vigorous effort to find people who appeared likely to have undergone many of the past significant social experiences which comprised the stages in the newly developed experiential process, but who still did not become dangerous violent criminals. In other words, I made a diligent attempt to find people who, according to this newly identified theoretical process, *should* become dangerous violent criminals, but who in all likelihood had *not* done so. The people I sought to play this pivotal function were domestic assault victims. This group was comprised of half a dozen recent women residents of a spouse abuse shelter, who had all been the victims of violent crimes, but who, with one important exception, had not reported committing any serious violent acts against others. The reason why this group of people was chosen to perform this vital function will become very obvious after the stages in the final experiential process are presented later in the book. The social experiences of this group of people, including the lone woman who had committed an assault for which she was not arrested, reconfirmed the need to make the revisions already made as a result of the earlier examination of the past social experiences of the young non-violent male group. This group's contribution was by no means redundant, however. The experiences of the domestic assault victim group and the non-violent criminal group did not completely overlap, so that they bore upon somewhat different points of the experiential process finally developed. Thus, for example, I found that the experiences of the single domestic assault victim who had committed a violent criminal act followed the same early pattern of sequential development as the young novices, except that her experiences occurred later in her life than in theirs. Thus, the final experiential process developed was ultimately confirmed rather than disconfirmed by the social experiences of the people in this last group, which provided me with the extra confidence I needed to conclude that I had finally developed the experiential process which creates dangerous violent criminals.

This final experiential process I formulated from the study of all these various groups' significant experiences consists of four separate stages: (1) brutalization, (2) belligerency, (3) violent performances, and (4) virulency. These four stages, which explain how people go progressively from being non-violent persons to becoming dangerous violent criminals capable of committing the heinous violent crimes described in the opening chapter of this book, will be described in the natural order of their occurrence in the following six chapters.

It should be borne in mind while reading these chapters that each stage describes the social experiences which people must completely undergo before they can enter the next higher stage of violence development. Until people have completely undergone a social experience, they have not *had* it. As John Dewey has lucidly explained in *Art as Experience*, one cannot be said to have had an experience until one has experienced the event, whatever it may be, in its whole or its entirety, rather than only partially.[8] Of course, it is only a matter of common sense that unless a social experience is completely undergone, its full impact cannot be felt.

4

Stage One:
Brutalization:
Violent Subjugation

INTRODUCTION

Brutalization is a composite experience consisting of three more elemental experiences: *violent subjugation, personal horrification*, and *violent coaching*. Although these three experiences are all different from each other in certain important concrete respects, on a more abstract plane there is a real and indisputable unity between them. They all involve in their own way people undergoing coarse and cruel treatment at the hands of others that produces a lasting and dramatic impact upon the subsequent course of their lives. Thus, these experiences may be thought of as constituting a trilogy.

Any discussion of the experiences in this trilogy must draw the widely known distinction between primary and secondary groups. Charles Horton Cooley is the originator of the notion of primary group. Credit for the complementary notion of secondary group is also usually given to him, although its progenitor is probably unknown. In his sociological classic, *Social Organization*, where Cooley directly described the primary group, he indirectly described the non-primary or secondary group:

> By primary groups I mean those characterized by intimate face-to-face association and cooperation. They are primary in several senses, but chiefly in that they are fundamental in forming the social nature and ideals of the individual. The result of intimate association, psychologically, is a certain fusion of individualities in a common whole, so that one's very self, for many purposes at least, is the common life and purpose of the group. Perhaps the simplest way of describing this wholeness is

by saying that it is a 'we'; it involves the sort of sympathy and mutual identification for which 'we' is the natural expression.[1]

Cooley later adds that 'Primary groups are primary in the sense that they give the individual his earliest and completest experience of social unity....'[2]

Cooley's conception of the primary group is most certainly how it should always be, but unfortunately, not always is in real life. Thus, what is needed is an alternative conception of the primary group which is not burdened by the unrealistic demand of displaying the social unity and harmony that Cooley gave it. A primary group may be more accurately defined as a group characterized by regular face-to-face interaction and intimate familiarity between its members, such as a family, gang, or clique, whereas a secondary group can be characterized by the absence of the quality of intimacy, such as a large school's graduating class. As will be seen, the key participants in two of the three experiences in the trilogy to be described are exclusively from the subject's primary groups, whereas in only one of the three experiences are they from either primary or secondary groups.

VIOLENT SUBJUGATION

As noted, one experience that subjects undergo during the brutalization stage is violent subjugation. During this experience, bona fide or would-be authority figures from one of the subject's primary groups uses violence to force her to submit to their authority. A bona fide authority figure may be thought of as a person whose superior status is duly recognized, even if only begrudgingly, by others, including her subordinates, such as the case of the relationship between a father and a teenage daughter. A would-be authority figure is a person whose superior status is subject to dispute by others, such as the case of the relationship between a husband and wife or a stepfather and stepson. Submission to authority figures requires not only obeying their commands, but equally important, showing the proper respect for them as superiors. When a subordinate is perceived as being disobedient or disrespectful, an authority figure may exert or threaten to exert extreme physical force in a brutal attempt to make the subordinate obedient and respectful. Subordinates often admit being disobedient or disrespectful to authority figures, but emphatically deny the right of authority figures to use brutal force upon them in response to their misconduct. Because authority figures use extreme physical force for the purpose of bringing the conduct of a perceived subordinate under their control, their use of violence has a strong utilitarian flavor to it.

Violent subjugation is practiced upon subjects in two distinct ways. One way it is practiced is through *coercion*. Here, authority figures employ violence or the threat of violence to force the subject to comply with some command (including to show respect) which the subject displays some reluctance to obey or refuses to obey outright. The authority figure may either first threaten the subject with battery if she does not comply with the command or else immediately begin battering her without giving any prior warning. In the event that the threat is not heeded or no threat is issued at all, the authority figure begins battering the subject. The battery is continued until the subject signals submission by either obeying the command or loudly proclaiming an intention to do so quickly. Since the authority figure continues the battery only until the subject signals her submission, coercive subjugation is brutal, but at least can be halted at the prerogative of the subject.

The typical course which the experience of coercive subjugation runs is as follows. Prior to the onset of the battery and even to its early stages, the subject may act defiantly, but as the battery continues and becomes more severe, the subject's defiance erodes into fear. The subject's fear steadily heightens with the continuation of the battery until it finally erupts into full-fledged terror, and panic sets in. The subject has now reached the point of breaking. The question which the subject always asks herself is: 'How much more battering can I endure?' to which she sooner or later answers 'no more'. The subject has now passed the breaking point, and submission appears to be the only way out. At first, submitting, and stopping the battery which it brings, provides a great sense of relief to the subject, but that relief quickly turns into humiliation with the realization that she was brutally beaten into submission. The humiliation from being brutally beaten down incenses the subject. Her burning rage becomes cooled only later when it is transformed into a desire for revenge. The subject's desire for vengeance expresses itself in passing fantasies in which she batters, maims, tortures, or murders her subjugator.

The experience of coercive subjugation is illustrated by the two cases below. In these cases, the subjects are both males in their mid-teens who were most recently convicted of armed robbery. The subjugator in the first case is the subject's stepfather, and in the second case it is the subject's father.

Case 12

I was helping my stepfather build an addition to our house. He told me to buggy the wheelbarrow with cement back and forth to the foundation. The wheelbarrow was so heavy that I could barely keep it from tipping over and was spilling cement all over the ground. He kept yelling, 'Goddamn it, stop spilling the cement. We don't have enough.' I was tired, hot, and sweaty, so I took a little rest after I pushed the wheelbarrow up to the foundation. My stepfather said, 'Don't just stand there; pick up the damn shovel and shovel that cement into the hole.' I got mad and said, 'I've had it with this crap. I am not doing any more.' He said, 'Why you little fucker, you better pick up that shovel.' He then gave me a chop in the middle of my back. When I started to walk off, he backhanded me under the jaw and the back of my head slammed into the house. I saw stars. He almost knocked me out. My head was hurting bad and I was scared he might hit me like that again. I said, 'Look, I'm real tired, I'm real tired.' He said, 'You better get your lazy ass back to work.' I got back to work, but I felt humiliated by what he did to me. The first chance I got, I ran off. After I ran off, I kept thinking about what he had done to me and got madder and madder about it. He wasn't even my real father and had no right to hit me. I wanted to kill him for it. I thought a long time about getting an equalizer – my baseball bat or bow and arrow and fucking him up bad.

Case 19

I was sitting outside in a lawn chair one Sunday morning. My father yelled from the door, 'Go get ready for church.' I ignored him and kept sitting in the chair. I hated church. I couldn't stand listening to those sermons about sinning and going to hell. That kind of preaching got under my skin. I hated all those church people. Whenever they saw me, they would say 'Good afternoon, brother Tom.' I couldn't stand hearing those church sermons and that dumb crap from those fools every Sunday.

When I didn't get ready for church, my father came back out

and said, 'I thought I told you to get ready for church.' I said, 'I'm not going to church.' He said, 'Oh yes you are going to church, now get ready.' I said, 'I'm not going to church any more', and then he said again, 'Oh yes you are', and went beserk on me. He started hitting me with his fists in the face and stomach. I yelled, 'Leave me alone, stop hitting me, I am not going to church.' But he kept on punching me saying, 'You are going to church.' When I fell down on the ground, he grabbed me by the hair and started dragging me into the house saying, 'If I can't take you one way, then I'll have to take you another.' I was scared he would pull all my hair out of my head, and my head and face were hurting bad, so I said, 'Okay, okay, I'll go to church. Stop, stop, stop. Please stop.' Then he finally let go of my hair and we went into the house. As we walked toward the bathroom, he shoved me through the door and said 'Now get ready.' When I looked in the mirror, I saw that I had a black eye, swollen face and fat lip. I was ashamed to go to church looking like that. I got so mad and angry thinking about it that I hit the bathroom wall with my fist. What he did to me was plain dirty. I wanted to get even with him for doing it. I wanted to kill him and kept thinking over and over again while we were sitting in church about shooting him.

The second way in which violent subjugation is practiced is through *retaliation*. Here, authority figures use violence to punish subjects for past disobedience to them or for a present display of disrespect towards them. The subject may have disobeyed some past command which the authority figure only now discovers or else may fail to show sufficient respect for the authority figure while in his immediate presence. The subjects may compound their offense by combining the act of past disobedience with a present act of disrespect, as often happens when they are interrogated about some possible past act of disobedience. As a result, the authority figure may announce an immediate intention to punish the subject physically for insubordination or insolence, or may directly attack the subject without bothering to announce the intention beforehand. Of course, a formal announcement on the part of the authority figures is often not necessary since their reaction to misconduct can usually be foreseen.

The batteries that are administered during coercive subjugation are qualitatively different from those administered during retaliatory subjugation. In episodes of the former, the subjugator readily accepts the offers of submission on the part of the subject, whereas in episodes of the latter, he refuses to accept them. During coercive subjugation, the battery is continued up to the point where the subject signals her submission through immediately obeying some command or pledging to obey it, while during retaliatory subjugation the battery is continued well beyond the point where the subject signals submission through such acts as pledging future obedience, begging for mercy or forgiveness, or becoming completely hysterical. During retaliatory subjugation, the battering is purposely continued to the point where the subject is beaten into an apoplectic condition or the subjugator becomes exhausted, whichever comes first. Thus, while coercive subjugation provides the subject with the prerogative of terminating the battering at almost any time she chooses through signalling submission in the ways described, retaliatory subjugation does not afford the subject this precious luxury.

The course which the retaliatory subjugation experience typically runs is different and more complicated than that of coercive subjugation. Initially, the subject usually feels dread or defiance, rather than only defiance as she does at the outset of coercive subjugation. If overcome by a strong enough sense of injustice at the anticipation of being battered, the subject may openly express outrage for her violent subjugation and sometimes even her disdain for the subjugator. Otherwise, the subject immediately becomes preoccupied with thoughts about the pain that will be suffered from the battering, so that feelings of dread rather than outrage overtake her. In any event, with the onset of the battery, the subject's outrage or dread quickly gives way to fear. As the battery progressively becomes more severe, so does the subject's feeling of fear, until it finally climaxes into full-fledged terror, and panic sets in. As in coercive subjugation, the subject is brought to or very near the breaking point. The subject asks herself the same question during retaliatory subjugation as during coercive subjugation: 'How much more battering can I endure?' The answer which the subject sooner or later provides is, once again, 'No more.' If there is no escape from the battering of the subjugator, then the only other alternative is to submit. In contrast with coercive subjugation, the subjugator does not accept the subject's signal of submission and halt the battery, but cruelly and relentlessly continues it.

Once the subject realizes that the offer of submission will not be accepted, her feeling of terror changes into resignation. The subject bleakly concludes that nothing she says or does will cause the authority figure to stop the battering. As the feeling of resignation overwhelms the subject, her sense of time becomes greatly distorted so that the battering may begin to appear to be taking place in slow motion. As the battery goes on for what seems to the subject an eternity, she lapses into an apoplectic state. The subject, who has now become numb by the pain from the rain of blows, virtually stops all resistance and passively absorbs the punishment. While in this state, she experiences the battery almost as if it were happening to someone else rather than to herself. By the time the battery is finally brought to a halt, the subject has sunk into a stupor. As the subject slowly awakens from this stupor, humiliation at being mercilessly beaten down overcomes her, but the humiliation is only short-lived. As in coercive subjugation, it rapidly switches into a burning rage which is partly cooled when it is transformed into an intense desire for revenge against the subjugator. The intensity of this vengeance greatly exceeds what the subject felt during coercive subjugation. She has recurring fantasies about battering, maiming, torturing, or murdering her subjugator long after this one episode of retaliatory subjugation ends.

The way in which subjects experience retaliatory subjugation is illustrated by the following cases. The subject in case 15 is a male in his mid-teens whose latest conviction was for aggravated assault, and his subjugator is his stepfather. In case 29, the subject is in his early teens, was last convicted of armed robbery, and his subjugator was his mother. Finally, the subject in case 38 is a female in her late teens whose latest offense was criminal homicide, and the subjugator is her mother. Thus, these cases show both males and females in the roles of subject and subjugator.

Case 15

My little brother told my stepfather that I had called him dirty names. My stepfather walked in my room and asked, 'What did you call your brother?' I said, 'I didn't call him anything.' My little brother said, 'Boy, you are lying.' I said, 'Boy, I didn't call you a cuss word.' My stepfather said, 'I know you are lying, boy' and walked out of the room with a mean look on his face.

A minute or two later, he came back in with an extension cord in his hand. He grabbed me by the shirt, shoved me into the corner, and started slashing me with the cord. The first time he hit me, I shouted, 'You dirty motherfucker', and then he hit me again and I shouted again, 'You dirty motherfucker.' He hit me again and said, 'I make it possible for you to exist in this world, boy, and I can take you out of this world.' I said, 'You are not my daddy, you didn't bring me into this world and you have no right to take me out.' After I said that, he went crazy and started slashing me again and again and again with that cord. It felt like that cord was cutting a ribbon around my body. When I couldn't stand the pain any longer, I started crying and screaming as loud as I could, 'Please stop, please stop, please, please stop.' But he wouldn't stop. He only said 'Goddamn you boy, I am going to teach you a lesson that you will never forget.' Since he was a madman, I knew that there was nothing I could do but take it. I thought he would never stop slashing me with that cord. After a while, it hurt so bad, I couldn't feel or hear anything but could only see him swinging the cord with that crazy, wild look on his face. Finally my mother came in and told him to stop, that I had had enough.

I walked out mumbling to myself and crawled under the house where I stayed for several hours thinking and crying to myself. I felt bad. He shouldn't have beat me that hard with an extension cord. I got so mad, I wanted to kill his ass. I wished I had a gun to shoot him and thought about stealing my grandmother's shotgun. I wanted revenge any way I could get it. His beatings always made me think this wild stuff.

Case 29

I was sitting at the top of the stairs flipping through the pages of the Bible and scribbling in it with a pen. When my little sister came out of her room and saw me, she said, 'I'm telling Mama on you' and yelled, 'Mama, Johnny's writing in the Bible, Johnny's writing in the Bible.' My mother told my sister to bring the Bible down to her. After my mother saw it, she said, 'Come down here Johnny, you're going to get a whipping.'

She took me in the bathroom and told me to take all my clothes off. I took everything off except my underwear. After she hit me with the belt three or four times, she said, 'Take off your underwear too.' I said, 'Okay, okay.' Then she started slashing me all over my raw body. I screamed and screamed, but she wouldn't stop. It hurt really bad. I thought she was going to beat me to death. When I started crying and begging her to stop, she said, 'You must be made to be sorry for the terrible thing you did so that you will never do anything like that again.' She kept beating me saying, 'You must be made to repent, my son, you must be made to repent.' I could see her reflection in the bathroom windowpane. I could not believe how bad she was beating me. I knew there was no use in saying I was sorry to her any more. She had gone completely crazy, lost her head. After she got tired of hitting me, which seemed like two hours, she opened the bathroom door.

I walked out in a daze, completely naked in front of my sister. I had big blue welts all over my body. I felt completely humiliated as I walked up to my room. I laid on my bed crying and getting madder and madder. I looked out the window and saw the clothesline. I wished I could get that line and strangle her with it. I wanted to wrap that line around her neck and pull and pull and pull until I choked her to death. I wanted to kill my mother.

Case 38

My mother came home from work and asked me where my little brother was. I said, 'I don't know where he is.' She said, 'I told you not to let him run off.' I said, 'I didn't tell him to run off.' She said, 'You better find him; now get your ass out there and go do it.' After we finally found him, she said, 'Go to your room and take those clothes off. I didn't buy those clothes to beat on.' I dashed up to my room and stripped.

She came in my room and said, 'Take all your clothes off and lay across your bed.' After I took my bra and underpants off, she started hitting me with an electric extension cord. I got so scared that I jumped under my bed, but she shoved the bed up. I tried to run out the door, but she blocked my way and drove me into the corner. She beat me all over with the cord – my ass, back, arms, legs, and even my breasts. She hit me everywhere except for my crotch. It hurt bad, and I screamed and screamed, but it didn't phase her. She didn't seem to give a damn how bad she hurt me. I thought she might beat me to death. I said, 'Please stop, please stop, I won't do it again, I won't do it again, I promise I won't, please stop.' She said, 'Bitch, I am going to teach you a lesson this time that your ass is never going to forget.' She kept hitting me and hitting me while I was jammed in the corner with no place to run or hide. Since I realized then that she wanted to straight-out hurt me, I stopped begging, screaming, and crying. I just looked at her while she beat me. She had a crazy look on her face. It seemed like she was determined to keep beating me as long as she could. It felt like I had been jammed in that corner for hours. I kept saying to myself, 'When is she ever going to stop, when is she ever going to stop?' My body felt numb with pain. Then suddenly she stopped and said, 'Bitch, you are going to school tomorrow with stripes.' Thinking about it made me feel ashamed. After she left my room, I asked myself, ' What mother would want to make her daughter suffer in agony like that for what I did?' I kept thinking I didn't deserve it.

As I was thinking about all these things, she called me down to wash the dishes. While I washed the dishes, I could see her in the living room listening to the stereo with her headset on. The anger started swelling up in me. I thought, I could just run in there with the knife that I was washing and chop her head off and she would never know it. I would tell myself, 'Do it, do it.' Then, 'Don't do it', then, 'do it' again.

In short, authority figures practice coercive and retaliatory subjugation differently in order to achieve their somewhat different goals. The goal of coercive subjugation is only to achieve momentary submission on the part of the subject and compliance with some present command. The goal of retaliatory subjugation is to achieve a more permanent state of submissiveness on the part of the subject and thereby ensure his future obedience and respect. Thus, while the batteries administered during retaliatory subjugation are done for their *long-term* effect, those administered or *only threatened* during coercive subjugation are done for their *short-run* effect. This explains why the batteries administered during retaliatory subjugation are less merciful than those administered during coercive subjugation, although both can be extremely brutal.

Moreover, while violent subjugation has been described as a *fait accompli*, in reality there are episodes of both coercive and retaliatory subjugation which are embarked upon but never successfully completed. The subjects may escape, or a third party may intervene before an authority figure can beat the subject into submission or even worse, an apoplectic condition. Authority figures may also come to the belated conclusion that the use of battery for the purpose of subjugation is an exercise in futility which can often have the reverse effect than the one intended. Finally, of course, the subject may eventually forcibly resist the violent subjugation, thereby changing it into a *violent personal revolt*, a special kind of violent performance which will be discussed in more detail in Chapter 8.

5

Stage One:
Brutalization:
Personal Horrification

A second experience which people undergo during the brutalization stage is *personal horrification*. In one very real sense, this is only the reverse of violent subjugation. Here, the subject does not himself undergo violent subjugation, but witnesses another person undergoing it. It must be emphasized that either seeing or hearing violent subjugation performed qualifies as having witnessed it. Paradoxically, hearing the performance of violent subjugation upon another person does not diminish the experience. It only forces the subject to listen more keenly to the performance than he otherwise might have and fill out the unseen portion with mental imagery.

Neither violent subjugation nor personal horrification customarily happens in a tranquil social atmosphere, but instead happens in a tempestuous one. Speaking less metaphorically, these experiences usually take place in a social atmosphere in which the interaction between the members of a primary group is pervaded by strife and friction and by the mutual distrust and ill-will that so often accompanies such interaction. If this mutual distrust and ill-will is allowed to become intense enough, then what Norman Denzin has appropriately called 'negative symbolic interaction', in which 'the actions and utterances of each member call forth violent and violence-repressed reactions on the part of every other member', may break out.[1] As Denzin explains, the importance of negative symbolic interaction is that it *promote[s]* the use of emotional and physical force to regain what has been slowly lost through violence – the sense of intimacy, closeness, and "we-ness" that [should] characterize all primary groups'[2] (emphasis added).

Although in the case of violent subjugation, subjugators are always from the subject's primary groups, in the case of personal horrification, victims are always from the witness' (i.e. subject's) primary groups, but the subjugators can be from either his primary *or* secondary groups. However, this does not mean that the victims' subjugators are equally likely to be from either the witness' primary or secondary groups. The likelihood of the witness knowing the victim well and the victim knowing the subjugator well, but the witness not knowing the subjugator well, is far less than all three of them knowing each other very well, since people who know each other well spend more time interacting with one another. Thus, the witness and the subjugator are much more likely than not to be members of the same primary group. Nevertheless, for the experience of personal horrification, the nature of the group relationship which exists between the witness and the victim is much more important than that which exists between the witness and the subjugator.

What gives the experience of personal horrification its personal quality is not just that the violent subjugation of another human being is witnessed in the same ugly fashion as it may have already been practiced upon the subject or may in the future be practiced upon him: it is also the special nature of the relationship which exists between the victim and the subject. The victim is always a member of one of the same primary groups as the subject. The victim is either some close relative of the subject, such as his mother, sister, or brother, or a very close friend. It is precisely the witnessing of the violent subjugation of a primary group member, as opposed to a secondary group member, which so deeply personalizes this experience and ultimately makes it exceedingly traumatic for the subject. I should point out that there is nothing particularly unusual about this, since the same thing is true in the case of death. The death of a secondary group member is much less traumatic to a person than the death of a primary group member.

Just as the subject can undergo either coercive or retaliatory subjugation, so can he witness either form of subjugation being practiced upon a fellow primary group member during the experience of personal horrification. As with violent subjugation, personal horrification is more fully and clearly experienced where physical force is actually used upon the victim than where it is merely threatened. However, in contrast to the experience of violent subjugation which took different courses, the course which the experience of personal horrification follows is virtually the same whether the subjugation witnessed is coercive or retaliatory.

The typical course which the experience of personal

horrification runs is as follows. Initially, the subjects feel a grave sense of apprehension as they detect that a nasty altercation between one of their intimates and a bona fide or would-be authority figure of their intimate is in progress or may soon start. The subject legitimately begins to worry about the physical well-being of the intimate should the intimate have to suffer the ordeal of total violent subjugation.

When the subject becomes aware that the authority figure is actually assaulting the intimate, his worst fears suddenly become realized. Confronted with the undeniable realization that the intimate is being physically and not just verbally attacked, the subject's initial feeling of apprehension about the intimate's safety gives way to strong feelings of anger towards the intimate's subjugator. The subject's attention now becomes riveted upon the assault itself, which is perceived almost as if it were happening in slow motion. Every blow of the subjugator and the victim's reaction to it is hammered into the subject's mind. The subject very soon begins directly or indirectly to ask himself the question: 'How much more can I let the victim endure before I do something?' The answer to this question, which he soon gives, is 'No more.' The wrath rapidly building up in the subject climaxes in an urgent and powerfully felt desire physically to attack the intimate's subjugator. This desire expresses itself in passing thoughts and fantasies about battering, torturing, maiming, or killing the subjugator.

However, the reality of actually physically attacking the intimate's subjugator, as opposed to merely contemplating it, quickly leads the subject to restrain his mounting fury. The subject swiftly weighs the chances of successfully prevailing in a physical altercation with the intimate's subjugator and the consequences to the subject should he fail. After soberly reflecting upon the chances of success and the personal risk involved, the subject's fear for himself steadily begins to override the fear for the intimate. The subject now finds himself trapped in an excruciatingly cruel dilemma not of his own making. He is afraid of what will happen to the intimate if he fails to intercede personally and of what could happen to the subject himself if he does intercede. This dilemma is only short-lived. The subject quickly draws the conclusion that he cannot possibly halt the violent subjugation of the intimate by resorting to physical force. This conclusion resolves the dilemma, at least for the moment.

Unfortunately, this resolution of the dilemma does not ultimately relieve the subject's great mental anguish, but only transforms it. The subject is now overcome with feelings of impotence which make the earlier feelings of anger return. But this time the anger is directed more towards the subject himself than toward anyone else, while before it was directed exclusively at the intimate's subjugator.

It is easy to understand why the subject suddenly switches the target of his anger from the subjugator to himself. He concludes, not unsurprisingly, that it was his impotence rather than the subjugator's wickedness which was principally responsible for the episode of violent subjugation which he only a few moments ago stood by and witnessed. No matter how right or wrong this reasoning, the end result is the same: he feels intense shame.

The cases presented below will provide a better understanding of the experience of personal horrification. In case 9, the subject witnesses his stepfather practicing coercive subjugation upon his mother, while in case 10, the subject witnesses his father practicing it upon his stepmother.

Case 9

One night I was woken up by loud voices coming from my parent's bedroom. I got a drink of water from the bathroom so I could find out what was going on. As I walked to the bathroom, I heard my mother say, 'No, I told you not to do that, I don't like it.' I thought to myself, 'What could he be doing to her?' I started listening as hard as I could. My mother said, 'Please don't do that any more to me, it hurts', but he said, 'I don't care whether it hurts or not.' I heard noises which sounded like scuffling and my mother screamed, 'Please stop, it hurts, it hurts bad, please stop now, no more, stop, stop.' She would cry for a while, scream out in pain, and then start crying again.

As I walked back to my room, I knew that he must be hurting her awful bad to make her scream like that. It got me so mad and angry that I wanted to kill him. I thought about going in there, pulling him off her and kicking his ass good, but he was too big for me to handle. I knew there was nothing I could do. I wished he would stop, but he wouldn't. As I heard her crying from my bed, I felt bad because I couldn't do anything to help her. I wanted to get him off her and hurt him, but I was too afraid. I kept telling myself that I was just a little sissy. Then I tried to fall back to sleep and pretend it was all a bad dream.

Case 10

When my stepmother came home from work, my father told her to go cook our supper since he was hungry, but my stepmother said, 'I'm tired, I'll fix supper after I take a shower.' My father then said, 'I'm the boss around here, not you. You cook supper when I tell you to. You are going to cook our supper now.' But she said, 'No, I want to take my shower first.' When she said that, I got scared that my father might try to show how macho he was.

After my stepmother told him that, my father said, 'Don't talk back to me, you bitch', and punched her hard in the breasts. She said, 'I'm leaving you for that. I'm going back to my mother's.' He said, 'You are not going anywhere, bitch, you are going to cook our supper.' Then he started pounding her all over with his fists. She put her arms up to protect her face and said, 'Don't Tom, don't do that, Tom, don't, stop.' But he wouldn't listen to her and kept on hitting her until she fell down on the floor crying. He got on top of her and started hitting her in the face with his fists.

I got angrier and angrier as I watched my father beating her. I loved my stepmother very much, and I couldn't stand to watch him hit her. I wanted to do something to him. The first thought that came into my mind was to grab the clock and bash him over the head with it. Then I thought about getting the butcher knife from the kitchen and chopping his head off. I wanted to kill him, but I was so scared that I couldn't do anything. I just stood there and watched my father pound her down on the floor with his fists for what seemed like hours, but was probably only four or five minutes. I became very mad at myself for not doing anything to him. Finally, I couldn't stand watching it any longer and ran out of the house yelling for help.

The two cases presented above illustrate how personal horrification arises from witnessing coercive subjugation. The two cases presented below illustrate how it arises from witnessing retaliatory subjugation. The subject witnesses his stepfather practice retaliatory subjugation upon his mother in case 12, while in case 22, the subject witnesses his stepfather practicing it upon his brother.

Case 12

I was babysitting my brothers and sisters while my parents went out. I was dozing off when I heard the front door open and my mother say, 'Thanks for the ride home, Carol.' About a half hour later, my stepfather came home, went to their bedroom, and slammed the door. Then I heard them begin arguing and got worried, so I went into the kitchen where I could hear better what they were saying. I heard my stepfather cussing her out for leaving without him when he told her not to or something. Then my mother said, 'Gary, quit cussing at me.' I heard slaps and clothes ripping and my mother crying. I got mad because I knew he was beating her. When I later heard screaming, 'Stop hitting me, stop hitting me', I said to myself, 'Oh shit, he's going to hurt her real bad.' I was so mad now that I wanted to go in there and do something bad to him. It flashed in my mind to kill him, to kill the crazy no-good bastard. I thought about getting a knife from the kitchen drawer and putting it in his back. I loved my mom more than anything in the world and didn't want anybody hurting her. I wanted to stab my stepfather so bad that it hurt, but I was scared that if I didn't kill him, he would really mess me up bad. I said over and over again to myself, 'Do it, don't do it, do it, don't do it.' One side of me told me to get the knife and kill him, and the other side of me told me that I better not try it.

As my mother screamed louder and louder, I got more and more desperate. I knew something had to be done fast before he hurt my mother real bad, so I called the police. For a long time afterwards, I felt bad about not being able to stop him myself from hurting my mother. I was angry at myself because I didn't have enough nerve to do what I wanted to do – kill him.

Case 22

My sister and I heard my older brother and stepfather arguing and got worried. Although my stepfather never hit my mother or sisters, he would hit my older brother and me. When we went into the living room to see what was going on, my stepfather had an electrical extension cord in his hand and was shouting, 'I'm sick and tired of your smart-aleck talk, I'm going to beat your ass good, you damn punk.' Then he started lashing my older brother with the extension cord. As he lashed him with the cord, he kept saying, 'You damn punk, I am going to beat your ass for talking smart to me.' I couldn't understand why my stepfather was beating him like this. My brother was crying and screaming for help, but my stepfather wouldn't stop lashing him with the cord. I thought my stepfather had gone straight off and lost his mind. He was swinging the cord wildly, hitting my brother all over – arms, legs, back, and face. I couldn't stand to watch him do it. It seemed like he was never going to stop, and I got scared that he was going to hurt my brother bad. I yelled, 'Stop hitting him, you are going to kill him. Stop, stop.' When he wouldn't stop, I felt the anger explode inside me. I wanted to kill my stepfather. I thought about picking up something and hitting him with it, but then I got scared. I was scared that if I didn't kill him, he would go off on me like he was on my brother. I was mad at myself for wanting to do something to my stepfather but being too scared to do it. I didn't know what I should do.

I knew somebody had to do something fast, so I ran out looking for my mother. After I found her, we ran back into the living room, and she said, 'Don't you do that boy like that, stop whipping him right now.' But my stepfather still wouldn't stop, even though it already seemed like he had lashed him with that cord for more than an hour. My stepfather had totally gone off, and my mother had to grab a hold of him before he would stop whipping my brother. Afterwards, my little brothers and sisters, who were sitting together crying and shaking, asked me, 'Will he do us like that too?'

According to conventional wisdom, there is always an enormous difference between undergoing an experience oneself and experiencing someone else undergoing it. However, the conclusion should not be drawn that undergoing violent subjugation has a greater impact upon a person than undergoing personal horrification. The worst part of *both* of these odious experiences is the twisted feelings and thoughts which can linger on in a disordered state long after the immediate experiences which generated them cease. Thus, although the experience of personal horrification may be less traumatizing than violent subjugation from a *physical* standpoint, it is not less traumatizing from a *psychological* standpoint.

Although these two experiences have been separately described, there can often be a subtle, but important interplay between them. After subordinates have undergone personal horrification, the mere threat of the use of similar physical force against them by the *same* authority figure may be enough to achieve their violent subjugation. This important observation explains why people can sometimes undergo violent subjugation without themselves ever being physically harmed.

In short, the harmful repercussions which can potentially flow in the wake of the combined experiences of violent subjugation and personal horrification are far greater than any one of them alone. However as will soon be seen, the full potential of this combination is not reached until it is further combined with violent coaching, the third experience in the brutalization trilogy.

6

Stage One:
Brutalization:
Violent Coaching

A final experience that subjects undergo during the brutalization stage is violent coaching. During the course of this experience, the subject is placed into the role of novice, usually by an older person who puts himself into the role of coach. Violent coaching is usually a very informal affair where neither the coach nor the novice announces that they are playing these roles. No regular times are specially set aside for practices, but instead the coaching is done sporadically during the normal round of activities in which the coach's and novice's lives intersect with each other. Although violent coaching is informal and implicit rather than formal and explicit, the goal behind it – prompting violent conduct – is plainly obvious to all.

The role of violent coach is always played by some member or members of the subject's primary groups who, as result of their familial relationship, greater age and experience, or all three, believe they have at least the right, if not the obligation, to instruct the subject as to how he should and should not conduct himself in conflictive situations. Thus, the role of a violent coach is performed by people such as the subject's father, stepfather, mother, uncle, older brother, grandfather, or older, more worldly close friends. It is not at all unusual for a subject to have more than one coach at the same or different times in his life. Thus, for example, a father may be aided in his coaching by his wife and an older sibling, or a stepfather or older close friend may later take over this role for a natural father, often with zest. Of course, not everyone can effectively play the role of a violent coach. As already noted, not only must the coach be an authority figure from one of the subject's primary groups, but the coach must also possess a special kind of credibility. Since many people, particularly men, often speak as if they are much more violent than they actually are, most people's violent proclamations are usually appropriately treated as idle boasts by others. Unless novices believe their coaches will attack or in the past have physically attacked people, the novices will not take their coaches' exhortations very seriously. Thus, subjects must perceive their coaches as being or having been authentic violent actors at the time of their instruction. This is not to say people who are not perceived as authentic violent actors, including authority figures, will not try to perform the role of violent coach, but only that they may not be very effective at it when they do.

During violent coaching, novices are taught the proper course of action to take towards people who provoke them. Their coaches teach them what they should and should not do when provoked by another person. Novices are taught that they should not try to pacify, ignore, or run from their protagonist, but should physically attack them. Further, novices are taught to use at least enough force to ensure that they will prevail in an altercation, even if it means gravely harming the protagonist. Violent coaching is based upon the stated or unstated premise that the world is inhabited by many mean and nasty people, both inside and outside primary groups, and the novice must be properly prepared to deal with these people when he meets them.

It may be beneficial to contrast what novices are *always* taught by their coaches with what they are *seldom* taught by them. Novices are always taught that taking violent action against a protagonist is a *personal responsibility* which they cannot evade, but must discharge regardless of whether they are a man or woman, young or old, large or small, or what their prior beliefs about hurting others may have been. On the other hand, what novices are seldom taught is an elaborate set of highly refined skills or techniques for attacking people. Thus, paradoxically, the emphasis of violent coaching is not upon supplying the know-how for gravely harming people but is upon conveying the realization that grave harm should be done to certain people. Violent coaching not only differs from the coaching done in conventional sports by the lack of regularly set aside practices for the novices, but also by the lack of a sophisticated formal training regimen.

Violent coaching can be profitably contrasted with its direct counterpart, 'learned helplessness'. Lenore Walker, who perceptively applied this idea to battered women, described the essence and importance of learned helplessness as follows: 'This concept is important for understanding why battered women do not attempt to free themselves from a battering relationship. Once the women are operating from a belief of helplessness, the perception becomes reality and they become passive, submissive, "helpless"[1] During violent coaching, the subject is taught to operate upon the direct opposite assumption that they should be forceful, dominant, and self-reliant whenever another person transgresses upon them. There is also a more subtle difference between violent coaching and learned helplessness which is easy to overlook. During violent coaching, the subject does not always *learn*, but is always *instructed* to be forceful, dominant, and self-reliant. It is only in keeping with common sense that merely trying to teach people about something does not guarantee that they will learn it.

A novice may be subjected to a wide assortment of techniques by a coach to prompt him to take violent action against people who provoke him. One technique which is used is *vainglorification*. Coaches may portray taking violent action against protagonists as glorious acts, directly implying that those who perform such acts are heroes, or at least anti-heroes. The way in which coaches glorify violence in the eyes of their novices is through telling personal anecdotes about their own or relatives' or close friends' violent acts. The anecdotes which coaches tell vary in their degree of development. On the one hand, elaborate anecdotes in which simple plots are actually developed may be told. The plots in these anecdotes follow a predictable course. A 'good' person becomes entangled in a physical altercation with an 'evil' person; then the good person subjects the evil one to a decisive and humiliating, but well-deserved, defeat. As expected, the coaches cast themselves, their relatives, or close friends as the heroes or anti-heroes and their adversaries in the altercations as the villains. The coaches may, on the other hand, tell personal anecdotes which are much more cryptic. They may talk about their own, their relatives', or close friends' past violent feats *as if* they are well known to everyone, so that telling about the circumstances leading up to them is unnecessary. Although novices may perceive a certain lack of modesty on the part of the coach in telling such anecdotes, this does not in any way diminish the glory which is attached to violence.

The teaching principle upon which this technique works is *vicarious enjoyment*. In the cases of both the elaborated and cryptic violent anecdotes, coaches speak about their own, their relatives', or close friends' violent acts as being true feats. Since novices draw a certain amount of pleasure from hearing about their coach's or other's violent feats, and perhaps imagining their own performances of violent feats, they relish hearing these violent anecdotes. The moral which novices deduce from coaches' violent anecdotes is simple: other people have achieved glory and become heroes or anti-heroes through performing violent feats, and the novices can do the same if they perform similar violent feats. Thus, of all coaching techniques to be described, this is the one which the novices find the least punitive.

An illustration of the way in which novices experience the technique of vainglorification is provided by case 20 below. The subject in this case is a boy in his mid-teens whose most recent conviction was for armed robbery.

Case 20

My father always told me that a man always fights his own battles and makes sure that he gets his revenge from people who fucked him over, but I hung around with two older guys who were like my older brothers. They talked a lot more than my father did about whipping up on people. Joe and Eagle would tell me about how they whipped people's asses for giving them shit – what they did to people who fucked with them for no good reason. They told me how bad they kicked this or that dude's ass and taught him a lesson he would never forget for fucking with them.

There was one story they told me that I will never forget. This one dude named Al fucked them over bad, so they both jumped on him and stomped his ass in the ground. After they stomped him, they dragged him by his hair into his house, dunked his head in the toilet, and told him to bob for apples. They said they really taught that dude a lesson he would not forget for the rest of his life. They talked like they got a lot of satisfaction from what they had done to him and were proud of it. Their stories about kicking people's asses always fascinated me. I wished I had my own stories about whipping people's asses and teaching them a lesson for fucking with me to brag about to people.

Another technique which coaches may use to prompt violent action on the part of their novices is *ridicule*. The coach belittles or threatens to belittle the novice for his reluctance or refusal physically to attack other people who provoke him. The means which coaches most often employ to deride novices is the *invidious comparison*. The coach will draw an unfavorable comparison between the novice and the coach or between the novice and some other commonly known third party whom the coach respects. As in the case of vainglorification, the coach will boast about his own or the third party's past violent feats. However, unlike the case of vainglorification, the coach will also cast aspersions upon the novice for not having any similar violent feats to brag about. The implication which novices draw from these comparisons is clear: they are not as worthy a person as the coach and thereby they deserve the derision.

The teaching principle upon which this technique operates is *torment*. If people are subjected to derision or the threat of it long enough because of their failure to perform some action, then the point will finally be reached where they will prefer to take that action rather than suffer further derision. Novices soon realize that unless the critical purview of their coach can somehow be escaped, they are confronted with the dilemma of either attacking their protagonist or being endlessly mocked by their coach. Since novices often perceive that the coach draws a great deal of intrinsic satisfaction from mocking them, they tend to take their dilemma more seriously than might otherwise be the case.

Case 2 illustrates how novices experience the technique of ridicule. The subject in this case is a man in his mid-twenties who was last convicted of armed robbery.

Case 2

> My father told me that there were two things I better always remember: 'If you ever get into it with somebody, don't ever run, but stand there and fight. If something is worth fighting about, then it's worth killing somebody over. If you get into a fight with anybody, try to kill them. I don't care who it is – a man or woman – pick up a stick, board, rock, brick, or anything, and hit them in the head with it. That way you won't have to worry about having any trouble from them later.'
>
> One day my father brought home some boxing gloves and told me to put a pair on. I thought we were only going to play. He started punching at me and telling me to punch him back, but I could never reach him. He said, 'You ain't shit, you little punk,

come on, hit me, you ain't shit. Anybody could whip your ass. I'm going to get your cousin over here to whip your ass. He's twice as bad as you are.' I felt frustrated and humiliated and started crying. My dad kept grinning, laughing, and punching at me and calling me a little punk. Finally, my grandmother heard me crying and came in and asked my father what he was doing. He said, 'I'm trying to make him become a man and not a punk. Since I'm his father, I've got a right to make a man out of him any way I want.'

Coercion, a third technique which coaches utilize to prompt novices to engage in violence against others, is nothing but a special case of the practise of coercive violent subjugation already described in the previous chapter. Some coaches threaten novices not with psychological punishment, as in ridicule, but with physical punishment. The teaching principle upon which coercion works is an old and simple, but effective, one – *fear*. The coach bluntly informs the novice that unless he physically attacks his protagonist, the coach will physically attack the novice with a vengeance. Novices thereby find themselves placed in the predicament of having to choose between certain defeat and sure physical harm at the hands of their coach or less certain defeat and thus only possible physical harm at the hands of some protagonist. Novices easily perceive that their coaches want them to draw the conclusion that it is far better to attack someone else than to have the coach attack them. Thus, it is clear to the novices that the coach is attempting to engender fear in them for their physical well-being in order to force them to take violent action against other people.

The two cases below illustrate novices undergoing the technique of coercion. In case 22, the subject is a boy in his mid-teens whose last conviction was for aggravated assault, whereas in case 38 the subject is a woman in her late teens who was last convicted of criminal homicide.

Case 22

My mother, stepfather, and older brother all told me the same thing. They said 'If you ever let people push you around once, then they will think you are a little bitch or pussy and run all over you. If you can't whip their asses with your hands, then pick up something – a bottle, rock, board, or anything, and hit them with it. Whip their ass anyway you can.' They also told me, 'If anybody ever does push you around, you better make sure you whip their ass or we're going to whip your ass. Would you rather whip somebody else's ass or have us whip your ass?' They told me that I better not take shit off people. If I ever did and they found out about it, I knew what they would do to me. They would whip my little ass good.

Case 38

My mother taught me to take up for myself when people bullied me or talked shit to me. She told me not to take any shit from anyone and she didn't care who it was, a man or a woman. She said, 'If people are fucking with you, then jump on their ass. Don't ask your brother to do it for you; you've got to do it for yourself. It doesn't make any difference if you are a man or a woman. You've got to fight for yourself and not expect other people to do it for you. If it comes down to kicking someone's ass, I want you to do it right, understand? You go on and straight beat the shit out of them. If you ever come home crying because somebody has jumped on you, I am going to whip your ass bad. Do you want me to jump on your ass or are you going to jump on the person's ass who fucked with you?'

I heard my mother talk this shit since I was little, but I couldn't bring it into play until I was older, in my teens. It didn't dawn on me until then to actually do what she said.

Still another technique which coaches use to prompt novices to take violent action towards other people is *haranguing*. Here, the coach repeatedly rants and raves to them about hurting other people without ever belittling or threatening them or appealing to their pride, as in the previous techniques. The teaching principle upon which haranguing operates is *incessant melodrama*: if someone is told something often enough and with enough force and conviction, then it cannot fail but to convince them eventually. As interpreted by the novice, the message behind the coaches' ranting and raving is that they, or at least certain general categories of people which would naturally include them, should physically attack other people who provoke them. After repeatedly hearing the coaches rant and rave about hurting real or imaginary, past, present, or future protagonists, novices eventually have the message firmly imprinted into their minds. Although the coach may never directly instruct them to take violent action against any particular person, novices draw the unmistakable conclusion from the railing of the coach that they should physically attack protagonists. Since their coaches so often engage in these violent tirades, novices cannot help developing the distinct impression that their coaches derive a perverse sense of pleasure from hearing themselves rant and rave. Novices may often later find themselves, just like their coaches, ranting and raving about hurting other people, but without at first understanding the real meaning of their violent proclamations. Thus, novices often begin mimicking their coaches' conduct before they fully understand it.

The way in which novices experience the technique of haranguing is illustrated in the two cases presented below. In case 23, the subject is a boy in his mid-teens whose latest conviction was for armed robbery, while in case 37, the subject is a woman in her late teens whose latest conviction was for criminal homicide.

Case 23

My dad would always come home drunk, yelling and cussing about what he would do to people who fucked around with him. He would say, 'I'll whip their fucking asses, stomp their damn brains out, shoot the s.o.b's....' He told my mother, 'If I ever catch you doublecrossing me, I'll kill you, bitch, and the man who's fucking you.' He said to my sisters, 'Just let me catch any of you going out there and fucking anybody who has a dick in his pants, I'll beat you little whores and the man who is fucking you to death. I'm not having any sluts in this family.' He made the point over and over again to me that if I ever got into it with any s.o.b., to kill the bastard. He said, 'A man should not back down from anybody, but make people pay the consequences for fucking with him or his family and not be scared or worried about going to prison for doing it. Even if a man has to go to prison, he'll still kill or hurt an s.o.b. so bad, that the s.o.b. will wish the fuck he was dead. A man will not let people get away with fucking with him or his family.' Although my dad liked to talk this way when he got all het up, I know he meant every word he said because he later killed a man and got sent to prison.

Case 37

My mother and grandmother didn't believe in letting people run over them, but believed in standing up for yourself and fighting even if you were a woman. They didn't believe in letting anyone insult, bully, or threaten them. My mother and grandmother just wouldn't stand for people messing with them. They were bold women and would fight a man or a woman.

If they both told me once, they told me a hundred times that I better learn to stand up for myself. They said, 'You can't depend upon a man, a man is not always going to take up for you and may try to hurt you, so you better learn to take up for yourself. A woman has to act, not just react, when people mess with her.' My mother and grandmother told me this over and over again from the time I was nine years old until I left their house.

The final technique, *besiegement*, is where coaches combine all techniques except haranguing in their coaching regimen. Since the presumption is that the use of vainglorification, ridicule, and coercion together will prove more effective than using any one of these techniques alone to prompt novices to take violent action against a protagonist, the teaching principle upon which this technique works may best be described as *overkill*. During besiegement, coaches shrewdly hand out different social penalties and rewards with the sole purpose in mind of achieving the same goal: prompting violent action on the part of novices. Novices are forced to endure the pain and anxiety of ridicule and coercion if they refuse to attack their protagonists physically, while they are offered certain relief from this pain and anxiety, as well as the added pleasure of vainglorification if they do successfully attack them. In this way, the coaches can utilize a relatively potent combination of social penalties and rewards to overwhelm the novice and overcome any reluctance on his part to engage in violence. Because the social rewards and penalties that accrue in the case of haranguing are not plainly obvious even to novices, its use would not significantly add to and could perhaps detract from this powerful combination. Of course, coaches who have a predilection for using haranguing may be averse to using besiegement and vice versa. This may better account for haranguing's absence from the coaching regimen of besiegement than the lack of any added efficacy from its presence.

Case 25 below provides an illustration of how novices experience the technique of besiegement. The subject in this case is a boy in his late teens who was most recently convicted of criminal homicide.

Case 25

My father told me that I had to grow up and be a man like him and stop being a boy and taking shit from people. He said, 'If you're going to be a man, you have to stand up to people. I don't take any shit off anybody and neither are you.' He would say, 'Son, at ten years old I was whipping all the little pussies' asses in my neighborhood. By the time I was your age, I could already whip almost everybody's ass around. Shit, I could have whipped your little sissy ass all over the place. I will always be able to whip your ass. You're nothing but a little pussy, that's all you are, a little pussy.' Whenever my dad saw me, he would always say, 'Hey little pussy, what you doing?'

At first I didn't really care when my father called me a little pussy and said that I couldn't whip anybody's ass, but I got tired of hearing him brag about himself. After he kept on threatening to beat my ass and calling me a pussy for not fighting and telling me about how tough and mean he was all the time, it got driven into my head.

Subjects do not always undergo the same coaching regimen over their entire lives, but may experience different ones. The authority figures playing the role of violent coach may change over time. Thus, for example, a stepfather may take over the coaching of a novice from an older brother who, in turn, may have taken over from the natural father. The subject's new coach may prefer the technique of, say, vainglorification, whereas the previous one may have preferred coercion. Not only may the subject change from a coach who uses one technique to a coach who uses a different one, but he may retain the same coach who decides to change his coaching technique, especially if he felt it were not proving effective enough. It should also be remembered that the subject can have more than one coach at the same time, and each coach can use a different technique. Thus, it is possible, though perhaps not very likely, that a subject could experience all five of the coaching regimens. But, no matter how many coaching techniques are used upon a subject, the coaching experience alone is ultimately not enough for a person to complete the brutalization stage.[2]

BRUTALIZATION: CONCLUSION

As should now be abundantly apparent, brutalization is an odious and traumatic experience. That it is also a chaotic experience is less apparent. The trilogy of elemental experiences which comprise this composite experience – violent coaching, violent subjugation, and personal horrification – may occur at different points in the subject's life. Although it would certainly not be unusual for subjects to undergo violent subjugation and personal horrification on the very same occasion, they probably usually do not undergo these experiences simultaneously. Moreover, they seldom undergo violent subjugation and personal horrification on the same occasion as violent coaching.

Furthermore, violent subjugation and personal horrification can be undergone during entirely different periods of a subject's life than violent coaching, although rarely are violent subjugation and personal horrification undergone in different periods from each other. Subjects may undergo violent coaching at the same, an earlier, or even later time period in their lives than they undergo violent subjugation and personal horrification. However until they undergo all three experiences, the brutalization stage is not completed. Thus, the number of weeks, months, or years it takes to finish this stage is subject to great variation. Nevertheless, the great bulk of people, particularly males, seem to complete it by early adolescence.

Perhaps more important than either the amount of time the brutalization stage lasts or the exact age at which it is completed is the condition in which it invariably leaves the subject. Upon the completion of this stage, the subject is, not surprisingly, left in a confused, turbulent condition. The erratic occurrence of the experiences of violent coaching, violent subjugation, and personal horrification in his life undoubtedly add significantly to the trauma of the overall brutalization experience.

7

Stage Two:
Belligerency

In the aftermath of the brutalization experience, the subject is, not surprisingly, dejected by the events that have transpired in his life. He is deeply troubled and disturbed by the episodes of violent subjugation, personal horrification, and violent coaching he has experienced. The question which he repeatedly asks himself, but for which he never seems able to provide a satisfactory answer is: 'Why did all this happen to me?' In attempting to find an answer to this question, the subject becomes a bundle of conflicting thoughts and emotions. It is in this state of emotional turmoil and confusion that the subject enters the belligerency stage.

At odds with both himself and the world, the beleaguered subject becomes unusually reflective. He ponders the nature of humanity and more particularly whether or not civility exists other than in fictional accounts of social life provided in books and by schools and churches. He also begins to scrutinize closely his past and present human relationships for what they may reveal about how human beings *actually* conduct themselves towards each other, as opposed to the pictures of how they conduct themselves towards each other contained in fictional accounts of social life. After considerable thought, he concludes that there is a huge gap between the ideal and real way in which people interact, although he is unable to conclude with any certainty why this should be the case.

The subject's reflection soon returns from the lofty heights of philosophical speculation over the existence of humanity, which for him is a mental diversion, to the more mundane world of the source of his present anguish. Experiences as odious and traumatic as those undergone during the brutalization stage are not easily banished to some remote corner of the mind and then quickly and — forever forgotten. To the contrary, they leave a dark and indelible imprint upon the mind, an imprint with which the subject must come to terms. The need for the subject to take stock and come to terms with the brutalization experience is not any different from the need of most people to take stock and come to terms with other agonizing experiences such as the death of a loved one, the dissolution of a long and previously happy marriage, or a prolonged bout of unemployment.

As a result, the subject begins once more to brood over the experiences of violent subjugation, personal horrification, and violent coaching, all of which he has undergone against his choosing. However, in contrast with what went on before, this time his brooding is done with an explicit purpose clearly in mind. He wants to distill from these three experiences their larger general meaning for his *future* relationships with other human beings. The subject wants to discover the wisdom hidden in these experiences for how he should conduct himself henceforth towards the people he will encounter in his daily life.

Unfortunately, coming to terms with agonizing experiences is not an easy task for anyone, especially for persons who have undergone brutalization. Brutalization is a composite experience made up of three closely intwined but nevertheless distinct experiences. Each experience produces its own characteristic enduring effect upon the subject which, as earlier suggested, generates both similar and conflicting emotions and thoughts in him. Consequently, in order to come to terms with the overall experience, the subject must sort out the various emotions and thoughts generated by each one of these relatively unique experiences.

The experience of violent subjugation generates relatively enduring emotionally charged thoughts that combine a barely repressed sense of rage with vague notions about physically attacking other people. Unfortunately, these emotionally charged thoughts are directed not only toward the subjugator, but at other people as well. The subject somewhat erroneously concludes that if one person presently subjects him to violent subjugation, others may try to do so in the future as well, and that he may always be plagued by violent subjugation from one person or another. Depending upon how introspective he is, the subject's conclusion stems from a self-conscious or unselfconscious overgeneralization based only upon his experiences with his violent subjugator or subjugators.

The closely related experience of personal horrification also generates relatively enduring emotionally charged thoughts, combining a barely repressed sense of rage with vague violent ideas and also a sense of powerlessness. However, in this case, the emotionally charged thoughts are not directed towards the subjugator or even towards other people in general, but instead are directed towards the subject himself. The subject somewhat erroneously concludes that since he was unable to prevent a person for whom he cared from undergoing violent subjugation, he must be inadequate and thereby an unworthy person. Depending again upon his degree of introspectiveness, he may come to this conclusion either self-consciously or unselfconsciously. In any event, he later unconsciously makes himself, rather than other people, the target of his violent thoughts and angry emotions.

Violent coaching, the final experience in the brutalization trilogy, further humiliates the subject, if not in the short run, then in the long run. It may humiliate him in the short run since he may have earlier undergone the violent coaching technique of ridicule. However, even if this was not the coaching technique used upon him, it is easy to understand how the subject would feel humiliation and the self-deprecation which follows in its wake in the long run. He has been both brutally beaten down and an eyewitness to persons whom he deeply cared about being brutally beaten down. Yet he has neither stopped their violent subjugation, nor his own for that matter, although he has seemingly been given ample instruction on what action should be taken to stop it. The question which has been in the back of his mind for some time and which only now moves to the forefront is: 'Why have I not done anything to stop my own and my intimate's violent subjugation?' The answer which is hard to escape, try as he may, is that he must be an inferior human being.

Nevertheless, it is not until the belligerency stage itself that the subject's problem finally becomes fully crystalized in his mind. This problem may be stated in terms of a personal query which the subject may raise literally to himself: 'What can I do to stop undergoing any further violent subjugation and personal horrification at the hands of other people?' This agonizing problem has now grown to such an immense proportion in the subject's mind that a definite solution must finally be found.

The real solution that finally dawns upon the subject is to begin taking violent action himself against other people who unduly provoke him. The dawning of this belated solution after the subject has already undergone the ordeals of violent subjugation and personal horrification, not to mention violent coaching, takes on the guise of the sudden revelation of the real wisdom of the lessons earlier taught him during his violent coaching, but which only now does he fully understand and appreciate. It is *as if* the subject had earlier been partially deaf and has only now heard what his coach had been telling him all along: resorting to violence is sometimes necessary in this world.

The belligerency stage ends with the subject firmly resolving to resort to violence in his future relations with people. However, this personal resolution is still a strongly qualified one. The subject is prepared to resort to potentially lethal violence, but only if he deems it absolutely necessary for the well-being of his body and mind and if he believes he has at least some chance of success. Nevertheless, the subject has now reached the plateau in his development where he is ready and willing to injure badly or even kill someone, should the proper circumstances arise.

Case 14 below recounts how a male in his mid-teens whose most recent offense was aggravated assault underwent the experience of belligerency, while case 6 recounts how a male also in his mid-teens, whose most recent offense was armed robbery, underwent it.

Case 14

I still get upset when I think about all the things that happened. I can never forget the beatings that my father gave me, the beatings that I saw my mother and older sister take from him and all his loud bragging about what he had done to people. The things my father did to us made me feel ashamed and mad. It built my anger up and up until I got mean and crazy. I got so that I wanted to stay away from everybody and wanted everybody to stay away from me. I didn't want to be fooled around with by people. I told myself that if anybody fools around with me bad any more, I am going to go off on them. I was ready to kill people who fooled and fooled around with me and wouldn't stop.

Case 6

The beatings my stepfather laid on me, the terrible beatings he laid on my mother, and all the violent rhetoric took their toll on my mind. It inflamed me and made me want to go for bad. I was tired of always being messed with by people. I was ashamed of being weak and lame and letting people mess with me all the time. I didn't want to be messed with by people any more. People had messed with me long enough. If anybody ever messed with me again, I was going to go up against them. I was going to stop them from messing bad with me. If I had to, I would use a gun, knife, or anything. I didn't mess with other people, and I wasn't letting them mess with me any more. My days of being a chump who was too frightened and scared to hurt people for messing with him were over.

The way in which the experience of belligerency is undergone will also be described in cases 9 and 26, below. In case 9, the subject is a male in his late teens whose most recent offense was aggravated assault, whereas the subject in case 26 is a male in his late teens whose last offense was for criminal homicide.

Case 9

I was tired of people putting their punk trips on me, calling me a 'punk' and shoving me around. I didn't like people treading on me, and I wanted to scream at them, 'Don't tread on me, don't tread on me.' I was scared that people would be treating me like a punk all my life. I hated myself for letting people make me a punk. I was ashamed that I was a helpless cry baby who couldn't protect himself or his mother. I was being stomped into the ground both mentally and physically. I knew that I had to somehow dig myself out. I finally came to the conclusion one day that I was going to have to kick people's asses like I had been hearing from my stepfather. I was down and determined not to let my stepfather or anyone else make me out as a punk. I was going to make sure that no one treated me like a punk any way that I could. I was not out to make other people punks, but nobody better try to make me out as one either. I had had it. This was it, the end of being a sissy punk for me. I wouldn't have ever wanted to hurt people bad if it wasn't for this punk stuff. It was what made me turn mean.

Case 26

The beatings I took from my older brother set sparks off in me. What my father told me about not letting people run over me set off more sparks. Seeing people I cared a lot for get hurt set off still more sparks. All these things sparked me off, ignited a fire in me that wouldn't go out. I got to the point that I wasn't going to let people run over me. I had taken, seen, and heard enough. The beatings I saw and took demonstrated to me in black and white the truth of what my father had been saying: you need to be violent sometimes. There was no more room in my life for people talking crazy and hurting me any more. I was going to stand up and stop people one way or another from doing that to me. Whatever it took, I was going to do it. I wasn't going to be down on myself any more for not having guts enough to show people they can't mess with me like that and get away with it. No one has a right to talk crazy or hurt me, no one.

In short, during the belligerency stage the subject makes a *mitigated violent* resolution. He becomes determined for the first time in his life to attack other people physically who unduly provoke him with the serious intention of gravely harming or even killing them. This deeply emotion-laden resolution springs from the special way in which he was induced from the volcanic blending of the wrenching experiences of violent subjugation, personal horrification, and violent coaching to come to terms with his brutalization experience *as a whole*. Each one of these separate experiences made its own more or less unique contribution to the final combustible mixture, leading him to make a mitigated violent resolution. Although his mitigated violent resolution may not be a socially desirable one, neither is it a totally unreasonable one in light of the odious experiences from which it was born. In any event, the subject's mitigated violent resolution, once made, begins rapidly and steadily to influence his conduct toward other people, while at the same time, slowly but surely fades into his unconscious.

8

Stage Three:
Violent Performances

The subject, now belligerent, awaits only the proper circumstances to test his newly developed resolve to attack people physically with the serious intention of inflicting grave injury upon them. At this stage, the question which is buried deep in back of the subject's mind, continuously haunting him is, 'When the time finally comes, will I be able to hurt somebody bad or not?' Intentionally injuring another human being gravely for the very first time in one's life is not as casual a matter as those who have not seriously contemplated, much less performed, such action might believe. Of course, many people say things like, 'I'll kill you', but these statements are usually made merely to express their anger rather than their serious intention to harm another person. They are merely idle expressive statements which sometimes give the false impression that anyone who gets mad enough can kill someone no matter how meek and timid they may be. However, it takes more courage than may be realized to cross the invisible line which separates those who will from those who will not deliberately jeopardize or take human life. It must not be forgotten that when one jeopardizes or seeks to take a human life, his own physical safety, freedom, and psychological well-being are often placed at considerable risk. Thus, although the belligerency that recently erupted in the subject is ready to erupt towards others under the proper circumstances, he must still summon the courage to release it.

What is the proper set of circumstances under which the subject will direct his belligerence toward others with the explicit intention of gravely injuring them? As earlier hinted, at this point the circumstances are only those in which the subject is unduly provoked or suffers greater than minimal provocation. More precisely, the subject must suffer either maximum provocation or at least moderate provocation. Circumstances of no provocation whatsoever or only minimal provocation are not sufficient for a violent performance. As will be recalled from Chapter 1, maximum provocation occurs when a protagonist's actions place the subject or someone about whom the subject cares in imminent danger, whereas moderate provocation occurs when a protagonist's actions purposely and cruelly antagonize the subject to the point of tormenting him. Thus, during both maximum and moderate provocation, extremely provocative actions are taken by the protagonist towards the subject, so that the violent actions subsequently taken by the subject would not qualify as heinous violent criminal acts as did those described in the first chapter.

Of course, even after the subject is provoked to the point necessary for his violent performance, there are many real life contingencies which can easily forestall his actual performance. To mention only a few, the subject could come to the conclusion that he cannot possibly prevail against his protagonist and become paralyzed by fear; or some third party may unexpectedly intervene at the last moment, depriving the subject of the opportunity to test his wavering resolve; or the subject's resolve may not waver, but his protagonist's resolve does, leading him to stop his provocatory actions towards the subject. Thus, for these as well as possibly other reasons, the subject's violent performance is always problematic no matter how much he might be provoked.[1]

As important as the circumstances surrounding the subject's violent performance is the *immediate* outcome of his performance. There are several very obvious and some less obvious possibilities open here. Obviously, the subject can win or lose outright a violent confrontation with a protagonist. However, even decisive victories and defeats can vary in their gravity. A major victory is where the subject scores a clear-cut win and in the process inflicts grievous injuries upon the protagonist. A major defeat is simply the reverse. It is a decisive defeat when the subject sustains grievous injuries at the hands of the protagonist.

A subject could also have a 'no decision' or a 'draw'. These two outcomes of violent altercations may be more common outcomes than either clear-cut 'wins' or 'losses' of even little gravity. Although the difference between a victory and a defeat is clear, the difference between a draw and a 'no decision' requires some explanation. A 'no decision' is where the altercation never progressed to the point that any decision could be rendered as to who 'won' or 'lost'. The altercation was interrupted before any of the combatants could strike a decisive blow against and inflict grievous injuries upon the other. In contrast, a draw is where an altercation did progress to the point that such a decision could be made, but still no clear winner or loser could be declared because the combatants struck each other with an almost equal number of decisive blows and inflicted equally grievous injuries upon one another. In case 13, the subject, a male in his mid-teens whose most recent conviction was for aggravated assault, is maximally provoked and later scores a major *victory* over his protagonist. In case 21, however, the subject, who is also a male in his mid-teens and whose most recent conviction was for aggravated assault, is moderately provoked and later suffers a major *defeat* at the hands of his protagonist.

Case 13

My little brother and I were walking down to the store when this older guy came up to us. First he looked at my little brother and said, 'I need some money, punk, give me some.' Then he looked at me and said, 'Man, your brother better give me some money.' I didn't want my little brother to get hurt so I said, 'Go on home now, Tom. I'll take care of this.' After I said that, Tom broke and ran. The guy then got mad and said, 'Man, you shouldn't have told him that. He was supposed to give me some money.' I said, 'That's between you two', and he said, 'No, now it's between us two', and shoved me. I knew the guy could stomp a mud hole in me if I fought him using only my knuckles because he was a lot bigger and older than me. After he shoved me, I pulled out a knife and surprised him. Before he could do anything else to me, I sliced him across the chest. When I saw the blood running out of his shirt, I got scared. I thought to myself, 'Oh no, I cut him bad. He might die. I've got to get the hell out of here fast.' I threw the knife down on the ground and blew in the wind. As I ran, I kept thinking, 'Oh no, now I've killed somebody.'

Case 21

I was playing pickup basketball in the school gym. The same guy on the other side kept guarding me when I had the ball. Every time I dribbled or took a shot, he was pushing or shoving me. I got mad and said, 'Get the fuck off me, man.' He said, 'Tough, that's the way the game is played here.' When he kept on doing it, I knew he was trying to fuck with me on purpose. He wasn't guarding me close, but playing dirty basketball. When he later knocked me down from behind, I got mad and said, 'Man, you better stop fucking pushing me.' He said, 'Fuck you.' I waited for him to do it again. As soon as he did, I turned around and hit him four or five times in the face which made him fall down. When he got up, he ran and grabbed a folding chair and hit me across the arms and face with it, which knocked me off my feet. I was laying on the gym floor almost knocked out with my face cut wide open and my eyes swelling up. I never really knew before how bad you could get hurt in a fight with somebody.

There is one particular kind of violent performance that demands special attention – the *violent personal revolt*. The violent personal revolt has special trappings which serve to distinguish it from ordinary violent performances. In these performances, the protagonist is always a current subjugator of the subject or of a loved one of the subject. Since the subject is seeking to thwart either his own or a loved one's violent subjugation, his act is one of outright defiance against a perceived evil oppressor. As a consequence, the outcome of the performance takes an extra meaning over and beyond that of any ordinary violent performance.

In addition to the usual physical, psychological, and legal risks, the continuation of the oppressive relationship between the parties is at stake. If the subject wins, then he or a loved one may escape further oppression at the hands of the subjugator. However, the subject realizes that if he loses, his oppression may become far harsher than before the rebellion was mounted. In violent personal revolts, 'no decisions' and draws are much less common than they are in ordinary violent performances where less may be at stake. Thus, for the subject, violent personal revolts usually end as either the 'sweet victory' long yearned for or the 'bitter defeat' dreaded during past thoughts of defiance.

Both an unsuccessful violent personal revolt and a successful one are illustrated below. The subject in case 9, which illustrates the unsuccessful revolt, is a male in his late teens whose most recent conviction was for aggravated assault, whereas the subject in case

16, which illustrates the successful revolt, is a male in his mid-teens whose most recent conviction was also for aggravated assault.

Case 9

After dinner, we were sitting around the table talking about events in the newspaper. There was something in the paper about communist countries, and I said that I thought real communism would be a good idea. When my stepfather heard that, he got mad and said, 'Why don't you move to fucking Russia?' I said, 'If we lived in Russia, I would send you to Siberia.' Then he blew his top and yelled, 'Don't smart off to me' and hit me in the face with his fist, knocking me back in my chair.

I jumped up and ran, but he chased me. When we got to my room, he grabbed me by the shoulders, threw me against the wall, and knocked me down. Then I decided I was going to fight and said, 'This is it. I'm tired of taking all of your bullshit.' He stared at me and said, 'You are? Then why don't you do something about it, punk?' I said, 'Okay, let me up and I will.' As I got up, I reached for the knife I kept in my dresser drawer, but he kicked the drawer closed on my hand. I screamed and pulled my hand out of the drawer. Then he grabbed me by the shoulders and slammed me against the wall again, but harder. He knocked the wind out of me and I fell down on the floor gasping for air. He stood over me glaring and said, 'You had enough yet, punk?' I said real low, 'Yes.' He said, 'Are you sure you had enough, punk?' I got my wind back and said, 'No, I'm not.' He said, 'Do you want some more of me, punk?' I quickly said, 'No, no, no.'

Case 16

About a month after the last bad beating my uncle gave me, we were all at the supper table eating. I said something nasty, and everybody laughed except for my uncle and grandmother. Without saying a word, my uncle got up from his chair and dragged me into my bedroom. He said, 'Boy, I'm going to really beat the shit out of you this time.' I said, 'No you're not going to beat the shit out of me.' My saying that surprised him. He said, 'What did you say?' I said again, 'You are not beating the shit out of me.' There was no way in hell that I was taking any more beatings from him. When he reached for me, I grabbed a long thick stick which I had ready in the corner and cracked him hard across the hand. He grabbed his hand, shook it and said, 'Oh shit, I'm going to beat the fuck out of your ass now.' I cracked him across the knees and downed him. If I had to, I was going to kill him to stop him from messing with me. As he tried to get back up on his feet again, I cracked him over the back and then in the side of his head. He grabbed his head with both hands and screamed. I said, 'Motherfucker, don't you ever mess with me again.' I saw blood dripping over his hands and down his neck and got scared. I figured I must have messed him up bad and better get the hell out of there fast. I climbed out the window and kicked the turf hard.

Whether or not a violent performance is a personal revolt or not, the experience can have profound consequences for the subject's life. If the subject scores a major victory, there is always the possibility of his moving on to the next higher stage of violence development. A draw or 'no decision' on the part of the subject will keep him in a state of limbo in the present stage until he proves the strength of his resolve to be violent by scoring a clear-cut victory in some later violent performance. Thus, to no surprise, neither draws nor 'no decisions' normally produce violent performances which are consequential as far as the subject's later violence development is concerned.

However, a clear-cut loss, especially several major defeats in a row, places the subject's continued violence progression in considerable jeopardy. After suffering repeated defeats at the hands of protagonists, the subject may go in either one of two directions. On the one hand, he may completely question the wisdom of his earlier resolution to be violent and come to the conclusion that since he has little aptitude for violence, it was a mistake, for him at least, to have ever made this resolution. As a result, he sadly resigns himself to being a non-violent person in the future. In this case, the mitigated violent resolution which the subject had earlier made during the belligerency stage may either slowly wither away or perhaps become broken into conflicting parts, leading him to develop a personality disorder or psychosis of some sort.

On the other hand, instead of sapping the subject's belligerency, defeats can sometimes greatly strengthen it. In this case, the subject raises serious questions about his aptitude for violence, but does not have any real doubt about his resolution to be violent. He belatedly comes to the crucial realization that his apparent lack of aptitude for violence has more to do with the ineffective tactics that he has been using than with the strength of his resolve. He concludes not that he should refrain from getting into physical altercations with people in the future, but that he should resort to more lethal violence and resort to it much more quickly than in the past. The subject learns the hard way that lesson expressed in the aphorism, 'If something is worth fighting about, then it is worth killing over', and is somewhat perturbed with himself for not having learned this important lesson sooner. Thus, bitter defeats at the hands of protagonists can have the paradoxical effect of making the subject more determined than ever to be violent and furthermore to use more lethal violence more quickly during physical altercations with other people.

Case 3 below illustrates how the subject arrives at the critical realization that he must resort to more lethal violence and how this realization strengthens, rather than weakens, his resolution to be violent after suffering major violent defeats. The subject is a male in his late twenties whose most recent conviction was for criminal homicide.

Case 3

After I got my ass whipped bad a few times, I realized that being a loser was not where it was at. I didn't want to be a loser any more and get my ass whipped. I wasn't running from people. I didn't go for that. I learned that I had to hurt somebody bad before they hurt me. If I couldn't hurt them bad with my hands, then I would use a brick, rock, board, knife, or gun to hurt them. Since I was small, I usually needed more than my hands to hurt someone bad. I needed leverage. I don't care how big a guy is, a knife or gun will cut him down to my size. I wasn't going to hesitate any more to use leverage when people messed with me. There is no place in this world for the weak, so I was going to be strong. If every time you get knocked down you don't get back up, you are in trouble.

Arriving at the realization that one must resort to lethal violence is one thing. Acting upon this realization is another. It takes a certain amount of boldness and recklessness to quickly resort to lethal violence during a developing conflict with another human being. But the sheer profoundity of this realization, together with the renewed need for taking decisive violent action against a protagonist, hardens the subject's resolve. Case 21 below provides an illustration of a subject who acted upon his earlier realization that when there is a conflict which has strong prospects of degenerating into a violent altercation, lethal violence must quickly be resorted to. As will be recalled, this is the same male subject whose earlier major violent defeat was illustrated.

Case 21

My girlfriend and I were at a pizza parlor that had a pool table. I started shooting pool with an older guy who was there, and my girlfriend sat in a nearby chair smoking cigarettes and watching us. While we were playing pool, I noticed that this guy kept checking out my girlfriend. She was sitting in her chair backwards and he was staring a hole through her pants. I knew what he was thinking, 'This is one bitch I want to fuck bad.' I tried to get his mind off her and back on pool, but he kept staring hard at her pants and shaking his head. So I let him know that she was my girlfriend, but he wouldn't take the hint and kept staring at her ass and shaking his head. The next thing I knew he walks right up to her and straight out says, 'You sure got a real nice big ass.' When she didn't say anything back to him, he said, 'You know, you ought to leave that little young asshole and go out with me.' I was getting really pissed off now, but before I could say or do anything, he reached down and squeezed her ass. When he did that, she jumped out of her chair and said, 'Get your hands off my ass.' He said, 'Fuck you, you dirty little rag', and she said, 'Get out of my face.'

I got mad as fucking hell then. First he won't stop checking out her body in front of me, next he makes the remark about her ass, then he squeezes her ass, and now he calls her a rag. After he called her a rag, that was it for me. He had now finally gone too far, so I grabbed a pool stick, tightened my grip around the thick part as hard as I could, and swung it with all my might at his head. I broke the thin part of it across the side of his head, which knocked him off his feet. Then I quickly turned the stick around, jumped on top of him and started smashing him in the head with the thick end of the stick. I was fucking up the guy bad, blood was pouring out all over his head, neck and shoulders. Everybody in the pizza parlor then started screaming, 'He's gone crazy, he's gone completely crazy. Call the police.' My girlfriend started yelling at me 'Stop, stop, stop. You're going to kill him.' I threw the bloody pool stick down on the floor, grabbed her by the hand, and we ran out the door.

For Jean Piaget, 'praxis' plays an integral part in the intellectual development of children. In *The Child and Reality*, he argues that: 'praxis is not some sort of movement, but rather a system of coordinated movements functioning for a result or an intention'.[2] By way of illustration, he further explains that: 'the displacement of an arm which interferes in the act of putting on or removing a hat is not praxis; a praxis consists of an action in its *totality* and not a partial movement within this action'[3] (emphasis added). I would agree with this general conception of praxis, with the important added proviso that the subject must always be conscious of the relation between the goal of his action and the means he selected for achieving it. In other words, *true praxis* always involves self-conscious action on the part of the subject. If this more vigorous conception of praxis is adopted, then violent performances may be considered a special form of praxis.

In short, people make their original mitigated violent resolution from their tortuous contemplation about their past traumatic violent social experiences – violent subjugation, personal horrification, and violent coaching. However, the expansion of this resolution requires much more than mere contemplation. It requires successful praxis or the successful performance of the activity ultimately contemplated – violent action. Nothing expands a person's determination to be violent more than the repeated successful performance of violent action. The more successful the performance or the bigger the violent feat performed, then the more quickly the violent resolution of the person can be expected to deepen and widen. The reasons behind the expansion of the subject's presently only mitigated violent resolution will be explained in the next chapter.

9

Stage Four:
Virulency

The subject has now scored his first major victory or violent feat during a physical altercation, often only after experiencing many draws and 'no decisions', several minor defeats, and even possibly some major ones at the hands of various protagonists. He has now finally prevailed decisively over a protagonist whom he has grievously injured in physical combat. He takes a certain amount of personal satisfaction at having kept his earlier resolution to attack people physically who overly provoke him with the serious intention of gravely harming them. Although he feels temporarily filled with a sense of personal satisfaction at having proven his resolve, the notable violent performance which the subject has given will not *by itself* have any lasting and significant impact upon him. Before the performance can have such an impact, its full significance must be impressed upon the subject's mind. The job of impressing the subject with the full significance of his successful violent action is gladly performed by other people who, for whatever reason, always seem to take a perverse interest and pleasure in violence – all the more so when they know the offender or victim.

In the aftermath of the recent violent performance, many people may come to know of the subject's violent feat. Members of his primary groups such as his brothers and sisters, neighbors, close friends, as well as members of secondary groups such as acquaintances, school officials, the police, prosecutors, and judges may come not only to know of it, but to take an active interest in it. The opinions formed about his violent action by members of the subject's primary groups, especially friends, almost always ultimately have a far greater weight in the subject's shaping of his own opinion about his actions than those drawn by secondary group members, such as official authorities. However, the two are not always independent or at odds with each other. The opinions of secondary groups may often serve to support and reinforce those of primary groups and vice versa.

In any event, the subject becomes conscious that other people's opinions of him have suddenly and drastically changed in the wake of his violent feat. They no longer see the subject as they did before his latest violent performance, but they see him as a very different person. Somewhat to the subject's amazement, he is now seen as an authentically violent individual, instead of a person who was not violent or only possibly capable of violence only a few short days or even hours earlier.

At least some of the people in the subject's primary groups see him not only as violent, but to his great astonishment, as *mentally unbalanced* as well. For the first time in his life, he hears people describe him in complete seriousness, rather than in a jocular vein, as a 'violent lunatic', 'violent maniac', 'violent crazy man', 'madman', or 'insane killer'. The subject may be cast in these terms without the benefit of an official diagnosis from a mental health professional. However, such terms are not always pejorative, since acting crazily may only demonstrate that one has real daring and pluck, which to members of some primary groups, is a positive rather than negative attribute, but only if not taken to extremes. Nevertheless, when the subject hears these colloquial epithets being seriously used to describe him, he may at first find it somewhat difficult to understand and slightly discomforting, if not outright alarming. Although the subject has no reservations at all about being known as having pluck, he may for a short while have true misgivings about being known as really 'crazy'. The subject may also be more than slightly puzzled as to why some primary group members whom he had always previously presumed strongly supported acting violently towards one's protagonists now suddenly begin hedging their support in the face of his recent violent feat in which he did this very thing.[1]

Moreover, the apparent reason why these primary group members see the subject as mentally unbalanced stems from the degree to which he injured the antagonist. They may truly believe that the antagonist deserved to be hurt, but did not deserve to be hurt as badly as the subject hurt him. Thus, their conclusion that the subject is mentally off balance is drawn from the excessive amount of violence that he chose to use rather than from the decision to resort to violence *per se*. Stated more colloquially, they believe that 'he went way too far'. This explains the apparent paradox of why some primary group members, including those formerly serving as his violent coaches, may react with shock and dismay after learning about the subject's violent feat.

Because the subject is seen by others as violent and possibly mentally unbalanced, he is treated much differently now than before. People treat him as if he literally were *dangerous*. They act toward him much more cautiously, taking particular pains not to offend or provoke him in any way. Primary group members, as well as secondary group members, take such precautions in the subject's presence. For the first time, the subject keenly senses genuine trepidation when he approaches people whom he knows, or more precisely, whom he is aware know of him. Of course, the irony is that the feeling of trepidation which the subject now senses others feeling toward him is the same feeling the subject himself felt only a short time ago while in the presence of certain other people. The subject's sensing of trepidation towards him on the part of other people marks both the climax to the subject's experience of violent notoriety and the dawning of a new experience: *social trepidation*.

The subject has now reached the critical point in his violence progression where he has experienced violent notoriety and the social trepidation which it brings. Although the notoriousness and others' trepidation which the subject has only recently experienced were not entirely of his own making, the subject must now decide whether to embrace or reject this personal achievement of sorts. The answer to this question presents the subject with a paradox. On the one hand, notoriety denotes being well known for something bad. On the other hand, it is sometimes better to be well known for something which most people think is bad and few think is good than not to be known for anything at all. Although the advantages may not be well recognized, being known as dangerous does have its advantages. The subject is afforded greater power over his immediate social environment. Since other people begin to think twice before provoking him, the subject can freely interact with other people without worrying as much about provoking them, so that for the first time he may feel liberated from the violent oppression of others. Moreover, painful memories of feeling powerless and inadequate originally aroused during his brutalization and later his belligerence experiences still linger in the back of the subject's mind. This cannot help but make his newly discovered sense of power almost irresistible. Thus, the subject's answer to the question of whether to embrace or reject the violent notoriety is virtually a foregone conclusion. He only too gladly accepts his violent notoriety and the social trepidation that comes with it.

Upon the subject's decision to embrace his newly gained notoriousness, he undergoes a drastic change. The violent notoriety and the trepidation which it generates in others reverberates loudly in the subject's mind. As a result of these reverberations, he becomes overly impressed with his violent performance and ultimately with himself in general. Filled with feelings of exultancy, he concludes that since he performed this violent feat, there is no reason why he cannot perform even more impressive violent feats in the future. The subject much too hastily draws the conclusion that he is now invincible.

Blown up with a false sense of omnipotence, the subject becomes, in a manner of speaking, impervious to all later opinions and sentiments about his violent actions and, by inference, about himself that are not congruent with those he has already heard and wants to continue to believe. The ecstasy produced by his recent experiences certainly renders him incapable of seeing himself in less than sanguine terms, and furthermore, it renders others incapable of making him see himself this way as well. His pugnaciousness has swiftly grown to the point where he will without the slightest hesitation strongly rebuke anyone who would foolishly criticize him. Proselytizing him now would prove especially risky, since he could perceive the attempt as sufficient provocation for his taking violent action.

From the lofty heights of this new psychic plateau, the subject makes a new violence resolution which far surpasses the one made before the latest violent feat. He now firmly resolves to attack people physically with the serious intention of gravely harming or even killing them for the slightest or no provocation whatsoever, whereas before he had resolved to do this only if more than minimally provoked by someone. In making this later violent resolution, the subject has completely switched his stance from a more or less defensive posture to a decidedly offensive one. The subject is determined not to tolerate any provocation from other people, and, should the whim strike him, to provoke other people. He has suddenly been emboldened and made venomous at the same time.

With this last development, the experience of malevolency, the ultimate irony surfaces in the subject's life: he has now gone full circle from a hapless victim of brutalization to a ruthless aggressor – the same kind of brutalizer whom he had earlier despised. The subject, who is once again revelling in thoughts of his now proven courage and prowess, is blind to this ironic turn of his life. If the subject were suddenly to become aware of this irony, there is little likelihood that it would move him in any way to change his present path. He now relishes far too much the idea of being truculent, eagerly looking forward to the opportunity to treat others in the same brutal fashion as he was earlier treated. The subject has what is described in common parlance as 'broken bad' and, as a result, has become a dangerous menace to others.

With the achievement of malevolence, a social segregation process begins. The primary groups in which the subject previously traveled gradually and significantly change. Many of his former companions and even some relatives begin to avoid the subject so they do not have to endure feelings of physical intimidation while in his presence, whether or not they, in particular, need feel this way. Meanwhile, the subject may find that he is now a welcome and desired companion among malevolent groups for whom having violent repute is a social requirement. However, until this happens, social isolation may result. The subject may find that he is being shunned by some of his former primary groups and not readily accepted by new ones. Without new primary groups to fill the void created by the loss of former groups, the subject becomes the proverbial violent outcast and loner so often read about in the popular press.

The manner in which subjects undergo virulency is illustrated in the three cases that follow. In the first case presented, the subject is a male in his late teens whose most recent conviction was for aggravated assault. As may be recalled, this individual's case has been used many times before.

Case 9

After the stabbing, my friends told me, 'Hey man, we heard about what you did to Joe. It's all over school. Everybody's talking about it. You must really be one crazy ass motherfucker.' My girlfriend said, 'Wow, you stabbed that dude.' Finally things came together and hit right for me. My girlfriend and all my other friends were impressed with what I had done. I didn't really care what my parents thought. Everybody acted like nobody better piss me off any more unless they wanted to risk getting fucked up bad. People were plain scared to fuck with me. My reputation was now made.

I was in cloud nine. I felt like I had climbed the mountain and reached the top. I had proven to my friends and myself that I could really fuck somebody up. If something came up again, I knew I could hurt somebody bad. If I did it once, hell, I could do it again. It felt just like the first time I had gotten pussy. After I knew how it felt to get some, I knew I could get some more. Now I knew I could fuck somebody's world around, send them sideways, upside down and then six feet under. There was no doubt at all in my mind now that I was a bad son of a bitch, a crazy motherfucker. I could do anything, kill or murder somebody.

Now that I had reached the top of the mountain, I was not coming down for anybody or anything. The real bad dudes who wouldn't associate with me before because they thought I was a nobody now thought I was a somebody and accepted me as another crazy bad ass. I became a go-getter. I would go after people's asses for pissing me off in any fucking way at all. I meant what I said to people and said what I meant to them. They better listen to what I said because I wasn't playing games any more, but for keeps. I was ready to kill anybody who walked the streets.

In cases 30 and 33 presented next, the subjects are both males in their mid-teens whose latest convictions were for aggravated assault.

Case 30

Within three days, everybody in my neighborhood had heard that I fucked up somebody bad. They would walk up to me and say, 'Hey, Jake, I heard you really cut somebody up bad at the barbecue.' After I said that I did, they would say, 'All right, you really showed that dude. You'll never have to worry about him ever coming back at you now. You sure are one crazy motherfucker. Keep on rocking and rolling.' I had gotten an instant reputation.

After that, I noticed a big change in people. They wouldn't say shit to me. Nobody would fuck with me at all anymore.

People were just too scared to get me mad because they thought I was really a violent lunatic and would do anything to anybody. They would tell people who didn't know me, 'Don't fuck with Jake, because he will cut you up. He's not afraid to cut anybody.'

Although I knew a lot of people didn't think what I did was right, I said to myself, 'Fuck what they think. I'm proud of what I did.' I was glad that I stabbed that guy after the way everybody else acted. I had proven I was crazier and badder than most people in my crowd. I thought I was the baddest dude in the whole town as long as I had a knife, and I made sure from then on that I always carried one on me. I decided I wasn't letting anyone fuck with me any more, but I was going to fuck with them. I was ready to go after people and slice them wide open with my blade. I was ready to cut a person up in a minute.

Case 33

After I busted that dude's head open, the principal kicked me out of school for the rest of the year. The students all spread around that I had fucked up a dude real bad and sent him to the hospital, so the principal had to get rid of me. Everybody, my people and close friends, thought I had gone too far on the dude. They thought he deserved an ass-kicking from me, but not to be put in the hospital. They said, 'You shouldn't have done him like that. You went too far.' It tripped me out as much as them that I could hurt somebody that bad.

But nobody in the school or around my neighborhood would fuck with me after that. People said, 'James is crazy. Don't go heads up with a dude like that because he will fuck you up.' Most people made sure that they gave me plenty of space and stayed mellow around me. They paid more respect and said 'Hi' to me when I walked by.

People may have thought that I went too far on that dude, but I later knew what I did was right. It must have been right because nobody was giving me any shit any more. They didn't want to take a chance of going up against me and having the same thing happen to them. Before I put that big dude in the hospital, they would say things like, 'James talks a lot of shit, but I bet he is not really bad.' I showed them I was not all talk. I proved that I might not be big, but dynamite can come in small packages.

The way people acted made me come alive. It swelled up my head. I said to myself, 'If I put that big dude's ass in the hospital, then I could put any other dude on the street there too.' If any motherfucker out there talked or even looked at me wrong, I was ready to walk right up on him and see if he wanted to give me some. I was ready to throw down with everything I had. If a motherfucker loses his teeth, then he lost some teeth. If he loses his eye, then he lost an eye, and if he loses his life, then he lost a life. It didn't matter to me. The way I looked at it was that is just one less motherfucker this world will have to put up with.

During this stage, the subject made an *unmitigated violent resolution*, since he firmly resolved to harm other human beings grievously without the need for them to provoke him unduly. The expansion of the subject's emotionally charged violent resolution from his previous mitigated to his present unmitigated one results from his prior social experience. More precisely, it results from the special way in which he was only partly consciously induced by his earlier stock of social experiences to embrace wholeheartedly, rather than reject sternly, his violent notoriety and social trepidation and thereby undergo the culminating experience of malevolency. Making an unmitigated violent resolution is as tragic as it is deplorable, although in the light of its experiential evolution, it is understandable. As in the case of mitigated violent resolutions, an unmitigated violent resolution, once made, rapidly and steadily influences the subject's conduct toward other people, while simultaneously slipping slowly but surely into his unconscious.

In short, virulency is the last of the four stages in the experiential process which creates violent criminals. Upon the completion of this stage, the subject is ready to attack people physically with the serious intention of gravely harming or killing them with minimal or less than minimal provocation on their part. Now he will commit the heinous violent criminal acts described in the first chapter. Consequently, the added nefarious distinction of being not only a violent, but a *dangerous* violent criminal can now be rightfully bestowed upon the subject. With every new person upon whom this nefarious distinction is bestowed, the domestic tranquility of society becomes that much more endangered.

10

Theoretical Implications

When combined together, the four stages – brutalization, belligerency, violent performances, and virulency – yield a new theory for explaining how dangerous violent criminals are created in society. The source of the novelty of this theory ultimately springs from its method of construction. As will be recalled from Chapters 2 and 3, the theory was constructed from the actual study of the *social experiences* of violent and nascent violent criminals, rather than from the study of bio-physiological, social environmental, or both types of factors, as has been the case in virtually all existing theories of violent criminals. The great theoretical advantage of studying people's social experiences is that it integrates, rather than segregates, the factors playing upon them from inside and outside the skins of their bodies. Thus, a theory can be constructed which avoids the trap of chopping the sources of human conduct into two separate parts: body and environment. One practical advantage of doing this is that it leads to the construction of a theory which is more closely in touch with the reality of everyday social life and thereby can be understood by almost anyone. Laypeople can easily understand theories couched in experiential terms, whereas they cannot understand those couched in terms of mysterious bio-physiological and social environmental factors.

Although this new theory explains the creation of dangerous violent criminals as taking place through the passage of these four stages, the mere entrance into any one stage does not guarantee the completion of that stage, much less the completion of the process as a whole. The completion of each stage is contingent upon the person fully undergoing all the experiences that comprise that stage, and the completion of the process as a whole is contingent upon the person undergoing all the stages.

In order for a person to complete the brutalization stage, he must fully undergo the experiences of violent subjugation, personal horrification, and violent coaching. In order for a person to complete the belligerency stage, he must undergo the experience of protracted critical reflection about his prior brutalization experiences, which leads to the ultimate achievement of a special insight: resorting to lethal violence is sometimes necessary in this world of ours. To complete the violent performance stage, the person must undergo the experience of *at least one* violent feat after suffering perhaps many draws, 'no decisions', and even some minor and possibly major defeats. Finally, for the person to complete the virulency stage, he must successively undergo the two closely intwined experiences of violent notoriety and social trepidation, and the culminating experience of malevolency.

Moreover, if a person enters but does not complete the brutalization stage, he will not become a dangerous violent criminal. If he enters but does not complete the belligerency stage, he will not become a dangerous violent criminal. If he enters but does not complete the violent performance stage, he will not become a dangerous violent criminal; and if he enters but does not complete the virulency stage, he will not become a dangerous violent criminal. However, any person who does ultimately complete the virulency stage, and consequently the entire experiential process, will become a dangerous violent criminal. This remains the case regardless of the social class, race, sex, or age and intelligence level of people, as long as their degree of mental and physical competence is sufficient for them to perform a violent criminal act. Thus, the process described here for the creation of dangerous violent criminals is highly problematic as far as its completion, although relatively universal as far as its application is concerned.

The processual explanation for becoming a dangerous violent criminal summarized above bears upon a critical theoretical issue concerning the *continuity* versus the *discontinuity* of violent conduct in violent criminals' biographies. According to the discontinuity viewpoint, people without any violence-related experiences in their backgrounds whatsoever are capable of suddenly committing heinous violent crimes without any apparent reservations or moral qualms. On the other hand, according to the continuity viewpoint, people who commit heinous violent crimes always have some violence-related experiences in their backgrounds, although they may sometimes be deeply hidden from others and not apparent without a thorough and painstaking investigation of their biographies.

After all, official records, as well as superficial self reports elicited during surveys about violence-related experiences are notoriously inaccurate. There are many good reasons why people will not quickly or easily admit to official investigators such as probation officers, court-appointed psychologists, and child protection officers that they have undergone brutalization. Reasons include the justified fear of totally jeopardizing or further aggravating already strained primary group relationships, not to mention plain shame and embarrassment. Superficial self report surveys which are now so popular probably provide no more accurate information on the presence or absence of violent-related experiences than do the results of official investigations and psychological evaluations. One of the same strong motives for falsifying responses to official investigators also exists for falsifying them to survey interviewers: avoidance of shame and embarrassment. If, as Derek Phillips has reported in his book *Knowledge From What?*, large numbers of people lie on surveys about such innocuous matters as whether or not they voted, they would certainly be expected to lie in even larger numbers about whether or not they have personally been brutalized or have brutalized other people.[1]

The present theory does not give blanket endorsement to either the continuity or discontinuity viewpoints. Just as people who have never read a physics book do not make earth-shattering discoveries in physical science, people who have never had any prior violence-related experiences whatsoever do not suddenly commit heinous violent crimes. Nevertheless, in crime as in science, people may exhibit real creative leaps in their thinking, feelings, and conduct, although these leaps do not come entirely out of the blue because their past experiences make these leaps possible. Thus, although people's present conduct can definitely go well beyond anything which they have ever done in the past, their past stock of experiences provides the necessary ground work for their new conduct.

Thus, the emergence of violent criminal behavior in a person should be thought of as simultaneously continuous and discontinuous with his biography. Since his present violent conduct significantly departs from his past conduct, it may accurately be said to be discontinuous with his past *behavior*. On the other hand, however, since his past stock of experience provided the groundwork from which his present violent conduct emerged, it can legitimately be seen as continuous with his past *experience*. The seeming contradiction in this statement can be removed by drawing upon the present theory. The person who for the first time suddenly commits a non-heinous violent crime may legitimately be thought of as having engaged in a new form of conduct. However, this new conduct arises from his earlier passing into the violent performance stage after having undergone all the prerequisite experiences for that passage. Similarly, if this same person later commits a heinous violent crime, this may also be considered a new form of violent conduct on his part – but again, this new conduct arises from his earlier passing into the virulency stage after having undergone all the prerequisiste experiences for that passage. Thus, the present theory takes a middle path between the more extreme positions of the complete continuity and complete discontinuity theses.

Any time a processual theory is formulated, the question which invariably arises is at what age people begin and end their stages of development. Although the data from which the present theory was constructed do not permit a definitive answer to this question, it may be surmised that most boys start the process just prior to their teens, with at least some completing it before their mid or late teens. For women, the completion of the process at least may be much later. Another closely related question which invariably arises with processual theories is how much time it takes to complete all of the stages. In the case of the present theory, the data from which it was constructed do not permit any more definitive answer to this question than to the previous question. Nevertheless, it can be said with confidence that the process may be stretched out over a long period of many years or may be compressed into a short period of a few years. The theoretical possibility exists that the entire process could be completed in a few months, producing what may be called a *cataclysmic experience*. It is precisely this possibility which gives some shred of credence to the notion of violent discontinuity mentioned earlier.

The theory also provides a thoroughly social experiential explanation for the creation of dangerous violent criminals. Although it is plainly obvious that all the experiences which comprise the stages involve psychological processes that required physiological processes for their occurrence, it is much less obvious that they also involve a social process in which other people's actions are always implicated to some degree. As will be recalled, brutalization, the first stage in the process, is a composite of three more elemental experiences – violent subjugation, personal horrification, and violent coaching. It is plainly obvious that all three of these experiences involve in their own special way people undergoing cruel or coarse treatment as a direct result of the actions taken by other people. In the case of the second stage in this process, belligerency, it is less plainly obvious that the experience involves the actions of other people. During this stage, the person becomes belligerent only after he apprehends the larger meaning of his earlier brutalization experiences. Although this apprehension involves only cognitive and affective processes which take place solely within the person, they nevertheless were originally aroused by his brutalization experiences which, as just pointed out, are social in nature. Thus, the belligerency experience is also ultimately connected to the actions of others, although less directly than the brutalization experience. The third stage in the process, violent performance, is much more directly social in nature than belligerency by virtue of its requiring more than one person before it can take place. There must, of course, be a protagonist to provoke the subject's violent performance, and the protagonist's subsequent actions play a significant part in whether or not the performance ends in a draw, 'no decision', victory, or defeat for the subject.

Virulency, the final stage in the process, also stems from social actions. The first two experiences which comprise this stage – violent notoriety and social trepidation – obviously stem directly from the actions taken by other people towards the person in the light of his violent feat. The last experience which must transpire during this stage – malevolency – stems largely from the person's reaction to the earlier two experiences, so that it can ultimately be traced back to the actions of other people as well. Thus, the entire four stage theory explaining the creation of dangerous violent criminals is just as dependent upon social processes as it is upon psychological and physiological ones.

However, the conclusion should not be drawn from the indispensability of psychological processes in the theory that these processes are presumed to harden into psychological traits which endure across the larger violence development process. Psychologists have been caught up in a rather vain quest to discover the psychological traits which distinguish violent and nascent violent criminals from ordinary people for over half a century. This quest has been stymied in no small part because the psychological traits, or more precisely, psychological processes, which violent criminals manifest do not remain constant, but change as they undergo new social experiences over the course of their violence development. Take, for example, the so-called trait of low self esteem which psychologists have long associated with violent criminal behavior. As the present theory makes very clear, this is not an enduring psychological trait, but a passing psychological phase. Although people certainly do suffer from low self esteem during the early stages of the violence development process, should they later reach the final stage, virulency, they will suffer from exactly the reverse problem – unrealistically too high self esteem to the point of arrogance. It is for this reason that psychologists' quest for the discovery of distinctive psychological traits of violent and nascent violent criminals can easily become chimerical.

The theory provides a social experiential explanation not only of how violent criminals are created, but also of how they are reproduced to ensure that we always have a plentiful supply of new candidates to replace those who lose their lives, are sent to prison, or possibly undergo maturational reform. The particular stage in the process which plays the most important part in the experiential transmission of violent criminality is brutalization, which should come as no surprise. The older, superordinate members of a primary group may coach violence to, practice violent subjugation upon, and personally horrify the younger, subordinate members of their primary groups. When the younger, subordinate members of these primary groups grow older and become the superordinate members of new primary groups, they, in turn, *may* perform the same odious actions upon the younger subordinate members of these groups, thereby potentially transmitting or passing on violent behavior to another generation.

Although the experiential transmission of violent criminality in this manner may almost repeat itself endlessly, it must not be forgotten that in any particular case it is far from inevitable. As should be apparent from the description of the present theory already provided, brutalization alone does not make a person become a violent criminal, but only makes this result a distinct possibility which, prior to this experience, it was not. Thus, not all people who are brutalized go on to become brutalizers themselves. Furthermore, even people who do go on to become violent criminals may later become reformed as a result of undergoing pacifying experiences before they have had an ample opportunity to brutalize the younger members of still new primary groups.

Some very dangerous violent criminals refrain from taking violent action against their primary group members.[2] Thus, while the experiential transmission of violent criminality definitely happens through reproducing the brutalization experience across generations of primary groups, this reproduction does not occur uniformly.

To avoid any later confusion, it should also be made clear that the brutalization stage in the present theory cannot be equated with the notion of 'child maltreatment' (abuse) which has been examined in relationship to juvenile delinquency.[3] The trilogy of experiences of violent subjugation, personal horrification, and violent coaching that comprise brutalization are not equatable to the triplex of the factors of 'physical abuse', 'emotional abuse', and 'neglect' that are often viewed as comprising child maltreatment. The former are seen as taking place chiefly in primary groups, whereas the latter are seen as taking place exclusively in one primary group – the family. But much more importantly, this conception of child maltreatment is based upon the presumption that the sources of human conduct can be divided into separate realms of the organic body, the mind, and the social environment respectively, while the notion of brutalization, which is conceived here as a social experience, is based upon the opposite assumption that the sources of human conduct cannot be divided into these separate realms. As a consequence, the notion of child maltreatment further compounds the error of dualism spoken of in the first chapter, whereas the concept of brutalization escapes it altogether. It is also largely for these same two reasons that the notion of the experiential transmission of violence formulated here is decidedly different from earlier conceptions of this process.

As suggested at the opening of this chapter, the present theory provides an explanation of the creation and reproduction of dangerous violent criminals which is different not only from past theories of violent criminal behavior, but also from theories of general criminal behavior. This assertion can now be demonstrated by briefly comparing the present theory with labelling theory, a theory which provides a well-known *quasi*-social experiential explanation of general criminal behavior. Labelling theory represents only a quasi-social experiential theory because, although it was based upon some social experiential studies, its theoretical superstructure was recklessly elaborated well beyond what its empirical foundation could support. Since labelling theory is a general theory of criminal behavior rather than a specific theory of violent criminal behavior, some minor adaptations will be necessary to facilitate this comparison.

The major principle upon which this theory operates is social labelling, or what Frank Tannebaum, one of its first progenitors, aptly described as the 'dramatization of evil': 'the process of making a criminal ... is a process of tagging, defining, identifying, segregating, describing, emphasizing, making conscious and self conscious; it becomes a way of stimulating, suggesting, emphasizing, and evoking the very traits that are complained of'.[4]

According to labelling theory, people may be placed into one of two categories: 'primary' violent criminals or 'secondary' violent criminals. Primary violent criminals sporadically commit only minor violent crimes and would include the bulk of the members of our society, whereas secondary violent criminals would regularly commit heinous violent crimes and would include not only a small select group of people in society as a whole, but only a select group of criminals as well. When a label of 'dangerousness' is successfully applied to primary violent criminals, they become quickly transformed into secondary violent criminals and in due time commit heinous violent crimes.

The problem with labelling theory from the point of view of the present theory is that at most it only provides half an explanation of how people become secondary or, in the parlance used here, dangerous violent criminals. Labelling theory provides absolutely no explanation of how people *first* become primary or, in the parlance used here, nascent violent criminals, while the brutalization and later belligerency stages of the present theory do provide such an explanation. Instead, labelling theory denigrates the importance of providing such an explanation on the grounds that most people in society are probably nascent or primary violent criminals, so that the real problem is explaining the creation of secondary or dangerous violent criminals who commit the heinous violent crimes. Although this point is undoubtedly true, it produces indefensible obscurantism when wrongly used as a justification for ignoring the development process behind nascent violent criminals. Thus, for example, if the brutalization and belligerency stages of the violence development process identified in the present theory were brushed aside as insignificant, the theoretical process primarily responsible for the experiential transmission of violent criminal behavior over time would remain obscured.

Moreover, until a person completes the brutalization, belligerency, and violent performance stages, he has virtually no chance of entering into the virulency stage where he is first labelled dangerous and subsequently becomes a dangerous violent criminal. By its very design, labelling theory is unable to take into account that people are well along the path to becoming secondary violent criminals *long before* they are officially labelled dangerous. In sharp contrast with labelling theory, the present theory explains how people become nascent violent criminals and makes this an indispensable part of its larger explanation, rather than dispensable to the explanation. According to the present theory, if people did not become nascent violent criminals, they could not later become dangerous violent criminals, a premise which greatly elevates the importance of explaining how people become the former.

From the viewpoint of the present theory, incompleteness is not the only serious problem from which labelling theory suffers. By emphasizing the labelling of people as dangerous, (something admittedly very important which is taken into account in the present theory during the virulency stage) to the virtual exclusion of almost everything else, labelling theory also denigrates the importance of the violent acts which generated the labelling in the first place. Consequently, labelling theory offers precious few insights into the psychological processes and immediate situational dynamics which bring about the initial commitment of violent acts and the outcome of these acts necessary for the label of dangerousness to be attached later to the person. Instead of making the *early* violent acts of the subject problematic and thereby of crucial importance, as the present theory does during the violent performance stage, labelling theory makes the actual commission of these acts of only secondary importance, concentrating attention upon the subsequent labelling. It fails adequately to recognize that successful violent performances are significant achievements in their own right, whose theoretical importance is equal to, if not greater than, the acts of labelling which they may later stimulate.

Thus, it can be concluded from comparing labelling theory with the present theory that they are not in close agreement on any score save one – labelling people as dangerous is important in explaining the creation of dangerous violent criminals. But it cannot be made the paramount reality.

The comparison of labelling theory with the present theory makes a larger point than merely that the respective explanations which they offer for the creation of dangerous violent criminals are vastly different: it also demonstrates the inherent danger of making *experiential leaps of faith*. One should never formulate social experiential theories of human conduct from mere deduction from more general theories of criminal behavior, including quasi-experiential ones. The theories constructed from this method, no matter how artfully practised, can never yield a theory equivalent to one constructed from the actual study of the social experiences of the people for whose formation an explanation is desired. Thus, the development of theories which are not based upon the actual study of people's experiences cannot be justified simply on the grounds that it merely provides another method for developing theories which in the end are substantially the same as those which are based upon the actual study of their experiences.

In short, the theory developed here explains the creation of dangerous violent criminals as taking place through a *violentization* process comprised of four stages, each one of which is based upon distinct social experiences. Thus, this violentization process is from top to bottom a social experiential one. As will be recalled, the notion of social experience as used here integrates, rather than segregates, the human body with its social environment, so that factors playing upon people from inside their bodies and from outside in their social environments are not falsely separated into two different realms.

11

Policy Implications

To the extent that our violent crime control policies are guided by theories of violent crime rather than constructed without the help of any well-developed notions whatsoever about this problem, our policy makers have been at a great disadvantage. Few, if any, of our theories of violent criminals are based upon the social experiences which make them violent. Instead, they are based upon various bio-physiological and social environmental factors which are said to impinge upon them. Thus, our crime policy makers have not had at their disposal ideas firmly grounded on the experiences of the very people whose actions they seek to control in fashioning their policies. It is hard to conceive of how an effective violent crime control policy could ever be developed without resorting to any ideas directly grounded upon the actual experiences of violent criminals. This glaring absence of experientially grounded theories with which to guide the formulation of our violent crime control policies may be one reason why they have not proven more successful in reducing the problem of violence.

The present theory of how dangerous violent criminals are created affords an opportunity to develop a violent crime control policy based directly upon ideas which are firmly grounded on violent criminals' actual social experiences. However, I should first acknowledge an important reason why a comprehensive violent crime control policy cannot be adequately developed from this theory. The theory identified only the four stage process which *creates* dangerous violent criminals. It did not identify the experiential process that makes them later become non-violent persons after having earlier been violent ones. Although the development of a theory identifying this separate experiential process fell outside the scope of this study, one would obviously be needed in order fully to develop a comprehensive, effective violent crime control policy.

The present theory identified four stages in the experiential process creating dangerous violent criminals – brutalization, belligerency, violent performances, and virulency. Since entrance into a later stage is predicated upon the prior completion of each earlier one, each of the four stages, with the possible exception of the last one, provides an opportunity, though not an equal one, to thwart the person's next higher level of violent development and simultaneously the completion of the process as a whole. Intercession at the earliest possible stage is probably the most preferable, because it cuts off the violence development of the person at the lowest possible point with the least possible danger to the community. Because the experiences which must be undergone to complete each stage are not the same, the nature of intervention required to prevent their completion must also differ.

The brutalization stage presents an opportunity to prevent the creation of violent criminals at the very outset of the process where it would very likely do the most good. Of course, that the experience of brutalization is odious in and of itself is sufficient reason to warrant preventing people from undergoing this experience. As explained, violent criminals are continuously being created in society through the reproduction of the brutalization experience across different generations of primary groups. The older superordinate members of a primary group brutalize their younger subordinate members who, in turn, may become violent criminals when they grow older, perform the same actions upon the younger subordinate members of new primary groups, and so on. Thus, the most effective means of preventing the development of new violent criminals may be to stop the experience of brutalization from being passed on from one generation to the next.

The experiential transmission of the brutalization experience could perhaps be discouraged through a special education program. Too many men and somewhat fewer women hold much too broad a conception of their perceived right, legal or extra-legal, to attack people physically who unduly provoke them. They especially hold steadfastly to this presumed personal right in the case of primary group members such as spouses and children. One goal of the education program would be to disabuse these people of this presumed right. Among other things, it would have to make much clearer the limits of the legal justification for physically attacking anyone with the serious intention of grievously harming them. Another goal of the program would be to provide people with other, more appropriate means of resolving conflicts with primary group members than violence and with information on what steps to take in the event that violence is threatened or used in such disputes. In short, people would have to be made aware that there are new rules for resolving personal disputes in primary groups which do not include the use of violence and that there are real consequences for breaking the rules.[1]

The educational campaign just prescribed for discouraging the transmission of brutalization over different generations of primary groups such as the family may need to be strongly buttressed by the effective application of social control in order for it to have any hope of working. Otherwise, the campaign may strike people as only the pious spouting of empty words. Most of the brutalization which takes place inside primary groups occurs in the family. The intrusion of social control into the family raises the fundamental issue of the degree of privacy the family should be afforded and at what cost to the public good. Frank Zimring describes this issue below:

> If privacy has any physical locale in modern society, it is in the home, properly renowned as a haven in the heartless world. If privacy has any social focus, it is in the family, a set of intimate relationships that can only flourish when sufficiently protected from public scrutiny. But privacy can metastasize into a Hobbesian arena where the strong prey on the weak and the weak on the weaker still. Life's greatest moments occur behind closed doors. So too do some of modern life's most outrageous exploitations.
>
> A jurisprudence of family violence needs to confront the question of what aspects of private life are properly public. A coherent policy toward family violence depends on balancing the public value of privacy in family life against the social costs of exploitation and violence in unregulated family relations. In the political and social climate of the 1980s, this task is difficult and complicated.[2]

Unfortunately, it is beyond the scope of the present discussion to balance the conflicting values of family privacy versus the larger public good. It suffices to say here that unless the brutalization taking place in families is effectively stopped, the creation of potential dangerous violent criminals in society will continue. As long as people enter and complete the brutalization stage, the possibility of their later becoming a dangerous violent criminal always exists.

Belligerency, of course, is the stage which directly follows brutalization. If the brutalization of the person cannot be prevented despite our best efforts, then attention must be directed at preventing the experience of belligerency. More precisely, the people who enter the belligerency stage must be kept from ever completing it. Psychological counseling especially designed for this purpose would be needed. The counselor should seek over many sessions to help subjects gain the proper cognitive insight into their present state of turbulent emotions and cognitions stemming from their brutalization. More specifically, the subjects would be progressively led to draw an alternative meaning than the one they would ordinarily draw from their brutalization experiences and thereby would be prevented from making a mitigated violent resolution. Fortunately, at this early juncture in the subject's development, all his angry thoughts and hostile feelings are still somewhat disorganized, which provides the counselor with a real opportunity to help the subject reorganize them back into a non-violent perspective and avoid becoming belligerent.

Of course, the psychological counseling would have absolutely no chance of succeeding if the brutalization of the subject has not stopped. As long as the brutalization continues, it cannot but help to counteract any positive effects of the special counseling. Under these circumstances, the subject would be faced with a cruel irony: not only is his brutalization continuing, but he is undergoing 'treatment' to prevent him from becoming violent, while the person who is brutalizing him is not subjected to treatment or perhaps even punished for his brutality. Thus, for psychological counseling to work, the subject would either have to be removed from his prior interactional nexus or that nexus changed by removing or drastically changing the behavior of the person or persons most responsible for the subject's brutalization experiences.

The intervention strategy for people who have already become belligerent and have fully entered into the violent performance stage would have to be very different from the strategy for those still in the belligerency stage. Since the subject's belligerency is now firmly entrenched in him, psychological counseling, no matter how intense or prolonged, is unlikely to prove effective. The subject must now be made to lose the belligerency ingrained in him instead of merely prevented from developing it. This presents a more formidable challenge, calling for a much stronger intervention measure than mere counseling.

The stronger measure that is now needed is *special primary group resocialization*. The aim of this resocialization would quite obviously be to make the subject lose his recently developed belligerency and renege upon his new mitigated violent resolution. The assumption upon which primary group resocialization operates is that since traumatic social experiences originally undergone largely in primary groups are mainly responsible for the subject becoming violent, new social experiences undergone in an entirely different primary group can make the subject become non-violent again.

During his participation in this new *non-violent primary group*, the subject would, among other things, be taught how to view and react emotionally to future protagonists in more effective ways than physically attacking them with the serious intention of grievously harming them. Teaching effective non-violent ways of handling disputes with others could be done through a regimen of *non-violent coaching*, which could employ some very similar techniques to those employed during violent coaching (i.e. glorification, ridicule). The persons selected to play the role of non-violent coaches could be confirmed ex-violent criminals instead of confirmed violent ones as in the case of violent coaching. Of course, in order for primary group resocialization to have any chance of succeeding, it would have to be done under very restrictive conditions. The subject would have to become a long-term member of his new non-violent primary group and end his contact with at least certain members of his former violent ones, at least until their prior composition, which included violent subjugators and coaches, changed.

Perhaps what would ultimately prove more difficult than providing either the psychological counseling or the primary group resocialization would be finding the candidates in time for these intervention programs to be beneficial. Unfortunately, young people often do not come to the attention of juvenile courts until they have already progressed beyond either the belligerency or even the next higher stage, violent performance, so that the prime time for providing these two forms of rehabilitation have long since passed. However, much could be done to solve this particular problem if the schools were made to play a greater role than they now play in identifying seriously troubled youths. It is unlikely that most people in the belligerency stage would escape the notice of their teachers, since they would in all likelihood 'act out' in ways which would provide clear signals of nascent belligerency. When confronted with a belligerent student, teachers quite understandably often react in a negative manner, which ignites rather than defuses the student's growing feelings of belligerency by subjecting him to further harsh discipline and banishment from school. Banishing a student to the streets provides no solution to this problem, but only displaces it to another part of the community where violence development will more likely be hastened than halted. Although belligerent students should not be permitted to disrupt instruction, school officials and teachers must look upon these students as people needing special attention instead of ejection from their system. This is the opportune time for school officials to contact social service agencies to make a concerted effort to solve the student's problem before he becomes a dangerous violent criminal.[3]

With regard to the violent performance stage, there is, of course, one slight advantage to attempting to rehabilitate people in that stage over those still in the belligerency stage. The people in the violent performance stage usually stick out more and are thus even easier to identify than those in the belligerency stage. People who have been in the violent performance stage for any length of time have had several ugly physical altercations with other people. Some of these altercations may have ended in draws and 'no decisions', others in minor victories and defeats, and some even in major defeats. The occurrence of these altercations should provide a clear signal to anyone of the serious nature of the subject's problem and the need for immediate intervention. Moreover, if during one of his violent altercations, the subject should suffer a defeat, especially a major one, it would provide an opportune time for intervention since he would be unusually receptive to primary group resocialization experiences. In any case, it is absolutely paramount that the intervention be done before the subject's belligerency leads to his commitment of a major violent feat because that could then catapult him into virulency.

Virulency, the final stage in the experiential process creating dangerous violent criminals, provides not only the last but also the least useful opportunity for successful intervention in the experiential process that creates them. It provides the least useful opportunity for successful intervention not only because it is the final stage, with none remaining to fall back on should intervention fail, but also because few effective measures can be taken to prevent the person from undergoing the initial experiences of violent notoriety and social trepidation and the culminating experience of malevolence which comprise this stage.

The experience of violent notoriety stems from other people's reaction to the subject's violent feat. Any official intervention *after* a person has already committed a violent feat will usually only backfire since it will add to, rather than detract from, his violent notoriety and the social trepidation which he subsequently senses. Official reactions such as arrest, placement in detention, appearance in court, pre-sentence investigation, psychiatric evaluation, and so forth merely lead more and more people to the conclusion that the subject is not only violent, but perhaps more dangerous than they ever imagined.[4]

The experience of malevolence, which stems primarily from the subject's reaction to other people's reactions, provides only a slightly better possibility for successful intervention. Once a person senses his notoriety and the social trepidation which it brings and then feels for perhaps the first time personal potency, it makes him very resistant to reassessing the meaning of his newly discovered violent notoriety in a way other than one leading to the conclusion to be malevolent. The subject has become much too boosted up much too quickly for him now to entertain seriously any notions not consonant with the source of his present positive conception of himself. Success, even if faultily conceived and ill-gotten, is hard to argue against, especially when in the eyes of its achiever it has been hard to come by and long overdue. It must not be forgotten that while fame may be morally superior to infamy, their impact may be remarkably similar.

Thus, the subject would be far less receptive to non-violent primary group socialization of the type described earlier at this late stage in his violence development than during the earlier stages of belligerency or violent performances. The inclusion of subjects who had advanced this far in their violence development would undoubtedly seriously jeopardize the success of primary group resocialization programs through, at best, acting in a recalcitrant and rebellious way, and at worst, bullying and grievously injuring members of the group.

The final and difficult question consequently becomes what to do about the people who cannot be prevented from completing the virulence stage and thereby the entire experiential process for becoming dangerous violent criminals. These select few are the *most* dangerous violent criminals in our midst, because they are the very persons who will commit the heinous violent crimes described in the first chapter. As explained, these people are now, for all intents and purposes, beyond any immediate hope of rehabilitation. Realistically speaking, the nature of their past social experiences makes most of them unamenable to any currently devisable rehabilitation efforts. Of course, if the experiential process through which dangerous violent criminals become non-violent persons were known, then perhaps such a rehabilitative program could be devised. Until such a program is developed, society has little choice other than to segregate dangerous violent criminals from other people. Perhaps only time, the corrosive effects of major violent defeats at the hands of others, and the ever-diminishing satisfaction from achieving major violent victories over others, together with other much more salutary experiences yet unknown, will eventually make most of them finally receptive to rehabilitation efforts of the type previously prescribed for people who have not yet gone beyond the violent performance stage. In order for any rehabilitative program to have credibility, it must be based upon the sad recognition that some people, because of their past social experiences, simply do not make viable candidates for rehabilitation in the short run and should be confined *until* and *if* they do make a viable candidate for rehabilitation within some maximum limit set by the law.

For the sake of social legitimacy, rehabilitation programs must also go one step further and fully recognize that there are some dangerous violent criminals whose heinous violent crimes are so atrocious that their freedom cannot be restored no matter how much they have been rehabilitated, because to do so would represent an affront to humanity. In mind here are people who have committed repeated or extremely sadistic acts of mayhem, rape, infanticide, or criminal homicide. After people have repeatedly committed extremely perverse violent crimes such as these, society cannot take the risk of allowing them back into its fold. Since such criminals are usually incapable of being rehabilitated in either the short or long run with absolute confidence, the dilemma of whether or not to release them upon evidence of their rehabilitation should seldom arise.

The violent crime control policy outlined above is multi-faceted. It combines what is previously known in the criminological vernacular as 'general prevention' with 'selective incapacitation' and what I would call *selective rehabilitation*. General prevention refers to a policy which seeks to stop crime by stopping or at least curbing the development of new criminals. Selective rehabilitation refers to a policy which seeks to change *only* nascent criminals into non-criminals before they become hardened criminals. Finally, the policy of selective incapacitation is where criminals who already are or are becoming active hardened criminals are imprisoned in order to stop their anticipated victimization of members of society.

The different aspects of the multi-faceted crime policy being advocated here would not work independently of each other but would work closely together simultaneously. To the extent that our general prevention efforts fail, we must fall back upon selective rehabilitation, and to the extent that our rehabilitation efforts fail, we must fall back on selective incapacitation. The more that selective incapacitation must be resorted to in handling violent criminals, the more apparent it becomes that our selective rehabilitation programs are failing; and the more that rehabilitation must be resorted to in handling incipient violent criminals, the more apparent it becomes that our general prevention programs are failing. However, the skeptical and shortsighted conclusion now so often drawn, that none of the preventive or rehabilitative programs devised will ever work, should be strenuously avoided. The failure of preventive and rehabilitative programs signals the need to scrap these programs and replace them with new, more effective ones. In no case does it signal that no effective programs for prevention and rehabilitation can be devised and implemented, nor that such efforts should be scrapped altogether in favor of a policy based upon simple retribution. A retribution policy operates upon the simplistic assumption that criminals should be punished for the sake of punishment itself, and that the more severe their crimes, the harsher their punishment should be, or more colloquially, 'the worse the crime, the more the time'.

It makes far more sense to take steps to prevent someone from becoming a violent criminal and victimizing others than to insure his harsh punishment or imprisonment after the fact. Similarly, it makes more sense to take steps to rehabilitate a nascent violent criminal before he becomes a dangerous violent criminal who commits heinous violent crimes upon people than it does later to insure his lengthy imprisonment. Still further, it makes more sense to incapacitate a dangerous violent criminal for whom rehabilitative efforts are either inappropriate or have already proven to be a failure, than it does to take the chance of his seriously harming any more people. Thus, a priority is clearly placed here upon general prevention over selective rehabilitation, and upon selective rehabilitation over selective incapacitation.

In short, the rationale behind the violent crime control policy outlined is that our first line of defense against violent crime should be that of saving as many people as possible from beginning the experiential process which creates violent criminals. Our second line of defense should be that of saving as many people as possible who have already begun the process from completing it. Only our last line of defense should be one of saving ourselves and society from the people who have already completed the process.

The most unique feature of the policy I advocate is that it tailors the response of society to the development of the violent criminal. This represents a significant improvement over past crude policies that lumped all violent criminals together. Prior to this, the only distinction ever made was between violent and non-violent criminals, as if miraculously there were no points in between the two or no progression along the way from one to the other. Another relatively unique aspect of the policy is its strong emphasis upon prevention and rehabilitation, procedures which have fallen into disrepute in recent times. However, for such a policy to work in the future in light of its failure in the past, it must be much more refined than ever before and must be applied much sooner in the potential and nascent careers of violent criminals. The problem with past preventive and rehabilitative policies was that they were much too crude and belated in application and far too naïve as to who could and could not be helped by them. Unless we make an effort to develop further a policy along the lines suggested here, there may be little hope of stopping the creation of dangerous violent criminals.

Notes

Chapter 2: The Key to the Creation of Dangerous Violent Criminals

1. S. Mednick, V. Pollock, J. Volavka, and W. Gabrielli, 'Biology and violence', in M. Wolfgang and N. Weiner (eds) *Criminal Violence*, Beverley Hills: Sage, 1982, pp. 38–40. A very similar version of this theory appeared earlier in S. Mednick, 'A biosocial theory of the learning of law-abiding behavior', in S. Mednick and K. Christiansen (eds) *Biosocial Bases of Criminal Behavior*, New York: Gardner, 1977, pp. 1–4.

2. Mednick *et al.*, 'Biology and violence', p. 39.

3. Ibid., pp. 39–40.

4. A. Montague, 'Is man innately aggressive?', in F. Marsh and J. Katz (eds) *Biology, Crime and Ethics*, Cincinnati: Anderson, 1985, pp. 155–6.

5. M. Wolfgang and F. Ferracuti, *The Subculture of Violence*, London: Tavistock, 1967. M. Wolfgang first conceived the idea for this theory in his now classic *Patterns of Criminal Homicide*, Philadelphia: University of Pennsylvania Press, 1958, pp. 328–9.

6. Ibid., pp. 158–61.

7. A critique of the idea of subculture which includes many criticisms directly applicable to Wolfgang and Ferracuti's use of this notion is provided by G. Fine and S. Kleinman, 'Rethinking subculture: an interactionist analysis', *American Journal of Sociology* 85 (1979). After reading their trenchant criticisms, one cannot but wonder if this concept should not be replaced rather than only rethought.

8. Wolfgang and Ferracuti, *The Subculture of Violence*, p. 143.

9. S. Shah and L. Roth, 'Biological and psychophysiological factors in criminality', in D. Glaser (ed.) *Handbook of Criminology*, Chicago: 1974, pp. 104–5.

10. R. Lewontin, S. Rose, and L. Kamin, *Not In Our Genes*, New York: Pantheon, 1984, pp. 267–8.

11. Shah and Roth, 'Biological and psychophysiological factors', pp. 106–7.

12. S. Mednick, 'Preface', in Mednick and Christiansen (eds) *Biosocial Bases of Criminal Behavior*, p.x.

13. J. Dewey, *Experience and Nature*, LaSalle: Open Court, 1929, p. 230. G. Mead takes a similar, but less lucidly stated position on the unification of the human organism and social environment in *Mind, Self and Society*, Chicago: University of Chicago Press, 1934. Dewey provides a very succinct and easy- to-read overview of his philosophy in his *Reconstruction in Philosophy*, Boston: Beacon, 1948.

14. See: F. Ferracuti and M. Wolfgang, *Psychological Testing of the Subculture of Violence*, Rome: Bulzoni, 1973; F. Ferracuti, R. Lazzari, and M. Wolfgang, *Violence in Sardinia*, Rome: Bulzoni, 1970; and Mednick *et al.* 'Biology and violence', pp. 40–6; Mednick and Christiansen (eds) *Biosocial Bases of Criminal Behavior*, pp. 4–8.

Chapter 3: The Research Rationale and Strategy

1. Thomas Wolfe, *The Story of a Novel*, New York: Scribner, 1936, pp. 51–2.
2. See H. Blumer, *Symbolic Interactionism*, Englewood Cliffs: Prentice-Hall, 1969, p. 38; M. Clinard, 'The sociologist's quest for respectability', *The Sociological Quarterly* 7 (1966): 402. Although these are not recent works, they are even more relevant today than when they were originally published.
3. Blumer, *Symbolic Interactionism*, pp. 30–2, 127–39, 171–82. Blumer's critique of the quantitative techniques used in the social sciences today has never really been effectively refuted, although it has been effectively ignored. See also A. Cicourel, *Method and Measurement in Sociology*, Glencoe: Free Press, 1964, pp.7–38 and F. Znaniecki, *The Method of Sociology*, New York: Holt, Rinehart and Winston, 1934, part V.
4. Blumer, *Symbolic Interactionism*, pp. 36–40.
5. W. Beveridge, *The Art of Scientific Investigation*, New York: Vintage, 1957, p.140.
6. Wolfe, *The Story of a Novel*, pp.47–8.
7. Fortunately, I was able to draw upon my personal knowledge of several violent criminals' lives as a valuable resource for this study, but most of this knowledge was gained long before the inception of the study. See L. Athens, 'Participant- observation of violent actors and acts', in my *Violent Criminal Acts and Actors*, London: Routledge & Kegan Paul, 1980, pp. 95–6.
8. J. Dewey, *Art as Experience*, New York: Minton and Balch, 1934, pp. 35–57.

Chapter 4: Stage One: Brutalization: Violent Subjugation

1. C. Cooley, *Social Organization*, New York: Schocken Books, 1962 (1909), p. 23.
2. Ibid., pp. 26–7.

Chapter 5: Stage One: Brutalization: Personal Horrification

1. N. Denzin, 'Toward a phenomenology of domestic, family violence', *American Journal of Sociology* 90 (1984): 490. In this insightful article, Denzin offers one of the most penetrating looks into the larger world of family violence found in the voluminous literature on the topic. For a very similar, but perhaps even better discussion of this topic, see N. Denzin, *On Understanding Emotion*, San Francisco: Jossey-Bass, 1984b, pp. 167–200.
2. Denzin, 'Toward a phenomenology', p. 490.

Chapter 6: Stage One: Brutalization: Violent Coaching

1. L. Walker, *The Battered Woman*, New York: Harper & Row, 1979, p. 47.
2. As will be recalled from the second chapter, according to Mednick's theory, children become dangerous violent criminals because of their failure to learn from punishment to inhibit their aggressive impulses. However, according to the theory developed here, children become dangerous violent criminals in part because they are taught through the violent coaching techniques described (most of which have punitive aspects) not only to express their violent impulses fully but quickly to develop very strong violent impulses when unduly provoked by someone.

Chapter 8: Stage Three: Violent Performances

1. L. Athens, *Violent Criminal Acts and Actors*, London, Routledge & Kegan Paul, 1980, pp. 19–38.
2. J. Piaget, *The Child and Reality*, New York: Viking, 1973, p.63.
3. Ibid.

Chapter 9: Stage Four: Virulency

1. The very fact that some of the subject's fellow primary group members not only express reservations about his violent feat, but also raise questions about his mental balance, has an important theoretical implication. It casts doubt upon any theory of how people become dangerous violent criminals based upon the idea of violent values, such as the subculture of violent theory developed by Wolfgang and Ferracuti and described in Chapter 2.

Chapter 10: Theoretical Implications

1. D. Phillips, *Knowledge From What?*, Chicago: McNally, 1972, pp. 22–3.
2. L. Athens, *Violent Criminal Acts and Actors*, London: Routledge & Kegan Paul, 1980, p. 33.
3. See, for example: S. Brown, 'Social class, child maltreatment, and delinquent behavior', *Criminology* 22 (1984); R. Hunter and Y. Walker (eds), *Exploring the Relationship between Child Abuse and Delinquency*, Montclair: Allan Osman, 1981.

4. F. Tannebaum, *Crime and Community*, New York: Columbia University Press, 1938, pp. 19–20. The first fully developed statement of labelling theory appeared with the publication of E. Lemert, *Social Pathology*, New York: McGraw Hill, 1951; but the theory did not become an intellectual force in the field of criminology until H. Becker published his now classic book, *Outsiders*, Glencoe: Free Press, 1963. H. Finestone has provided the most profound analysis of labelling theory which exists in his little known but important book, *Victims of Change*, Westport: Greenwood Press, 1976, pp. 187–219.

Chapter 11: Policy Implications

1. Although using the mass media would be the fastest and simplest way for this education program to deliver its message to people, it might not be the most effective one. The principal problem with using the mass media for this purpose is that its effect upon people is almost always mediated by their daily experiences in their primary groups. It is during interaction with the fellow members of their primary groups that people decide upon the significance of messages delivered to them through the mass media. Thus, unless the primary groups in which violence is practiced were also re-educated by some other more direct means, the ultimate effect of a mass media campaign may not be as great as desired. See, for example: H. Blumer, *Symbolic Interactionism*, Englewood Cliffs: Prentice-Hall, 1969, pp. 187–8, 193; G. Fine and S. Kleinman, 'Rethinking subculture: an interactionist analysis', *American Journal of Sociology* 85 (1979): 11–12.

2. F. Zimring, 'Legal perspectives on family violence', *California Law Review* 75 (1987): 521.

3. Of course before these steps are taken, the student's violation of the school's conduct code must be properly established. M. McDermott reviews data from several different studies which provide rather strong support for the general argument made here. See 'Crime in the school and in the community: offenders, victims, and fearful youths', *Crime and Delinquency* 29 (1983).

4. Herein lies the grain of truth of the labelling theory of criminal behavior critically discussed in the previous chapter. It must be remembered that in order for labelling to have a crucial effect, it must occur at the proper point in the person's violence development.

Bibliography

Athens, L. (1980) *Violent Criminal Acts and Actors*, London: Routledge & Kegan Paul.

Becker, H. (1963) *Outsiders*, Glencoe: Free Press.

Beveridge, W. (1957) *The Art of Scientific Investigation*, New York: Vintage.

Blumer, H. (1969) *Symbolic Interactionism*, Englewood Cliffs: Prentice-Hall.

Brown, S. (1984) 'Social class, child maltreatment, and delinquent behavior', *Criminology* 22: 259–78.

Cicourel, A. (1964) *Method and Measurement in Sociology*, Glencoe: Free Press.

Clinard, M. (1966) 'The sociologist's quest for respectability', *The Sociological Quarterly* 7: 399–412.

Cooley, C. (1962) *Social Organization*, New York: Schocken (originally published 1909).

Denzin, N. (1984a) 'Toward a phenomenology of domestic, family violence', *American Journal of Sociology* 90: 483–513.

—— (1984b) *On Understanding Emotion*, San Francisco: Jossey-Bass.

Dewey, J. (1929) *Experience and Nature*, La Salle: Open Court.

——(1934) *Art As Experience*, New York: Minton and Balch.

——(1948) *Reconstruction in Philosophy*, Boston: Beacon.

Ferracuti, F. and Wolfgang M (1973) *Psychological Testing of the Subculture of Violence*, Rome: Bulzoni.

Ferracuti, F., Lazzari, R., and Wolfgang, M. (1970) *Violence in Sardina*, Rome: Bulzoni.

Fine, G. and Kleinman, S. (1979) 'Rethinking subculture: an interactionist analysis', *American Journal of Sociology* 85: 1–20.

Finestone, H. (1976) *Victims of Change*, Westport: Greenwood Press.

Hunter, R. and Walker, Y. (eds) (1981) *Exploring the Relationship between Child Abuse and Delinquency*, Montclair: Allan Osman.

Lemert, E. (1951) *Social Pathology*, New York: McGraw-Hill.

Lewontin, R., Rose, S., and Kamin, L. (1984) *Not In Our Genes*, New York: Pantheon.

McDermott, J. (1983) 'Crime in the school and in the community: offenders, victims, and fearful youths', *Crime and Delinquency* 29 : 270–82.

Mead, G. (1934) *Mind, Self and Society*, Chicago: University of Chicago Press.

Mednick, S. (1977a) 'Preface', in S. Mednick and K. Christiansen (eds) *Biosocial Bases of Criminal Behavior*, New York: Gardner, pp. ix–x.

——(1977b)'A biosocial theory of the learning of law-abiding behavior', in S. Mednick and K. Christiansen (eds) *Biosocial Bases of Criminal Behavior*, New York: Gardner, pp. 1–8.

Mednick, S., Pollock,V., Volavka, J., and Gabrielli, W. (1982) 'Biology and violence', in M. Wolfgang and N. Weiner (eds) *Criminal Violence*, Beverley Hills: Sage, pp. 21–80.

Montagu, A., (1985) 'Is man innately aggressive?', in F. Marsh and J. Katz (eds) *Biology, Crime and Ethics*, Cincinnati: Anderson, pp. 148–57.

Phillips, D. (1972) *Knowledge From What?*, Chicago: Rand McNally.

Piaget, J. (1974) *The Child and Reality*, New York: Viking.

Shah, S. and Roth, L. (1974) 'Biological and psychophysiological factors in criminality', in D. Glaser (ed.) *Handbook of Criminality*, Chicago: Rand McNally, pp. 101–73.

Tannebaum, F. (1938) *Crime and the Community*, New York: Columbia University Press.

Walker, L. (1979) *The Battered Woman*, New York: Harper & Row.

Wilson, J. and Herrnstein, R. (1985) *Crime and Human Nature*, New York: Simon and Schuster.

Wolfgang, M. (1958) *Patterns of Criminal Homicide*, Philadelphia: University of Pennsylvania Press.

Wolfgang, M. and Ferracuti, F. (1967) *The Subculture of Violence*, London: Tavistock.

Wolfe, T. (1929) *Look Homeward Angel*, New York: Scribner.

Wolfe, T. (1936) *The Story of a Novel*, New York: Scribner.

Zimring, F. (1987) 'Legal perspectives on family violence', *California Law Review* 75: 521–39.

Znaniecki, F.(1934) *The Method of Sociology*, New York: Holt, Rinehart and Winston.

Index

academics 20
assumptions behind study
18–21; depth over breadth
21; developmental 20–1;
experiential 18–20
authority figures 28–9, 31, 36,
40, 46

belligerency 57–62; illustrations
of 60–3; and mitigated
violent resolution 60–3; and
self deprecation 59; and
sudden revelation 60
besiegement 54; illustration of
55
bio-physiological theories 7–10
bitter defeat 66
brutalization 27–56; age at
completion of 56; chaotic
nature of 56; definition of 27;
duration of 56; interplay
between elemental
experiences 56; and later
intervention 91–3; primary
and secondary group
relationships 28, 38–9, 46; as
trilogy 27, 56

cataclysmic experience 83
child maltreatment 86
coercion 51; as special case of
violent subjugation 51;
illustration of 51–2
coercive subjugation 29–30;
illustrations of 30–1; in
contrast to retaliatory 31–2,
36; typical course of 29
constant comparison 23–4
continuity versus discontinuity
issue 81–3

dangerous 74, 87–8, 96
dangerous violent criminals 5–6,
79, 80–1, 87–9, 96–9; control
of 96–7; definition of 5; key

to creation 16–17; moral
ambiguity over 6
domestic assault victims 24–5
"dramatization of evil" 87
draw 64–5
dualism 13–17, 19, 86

educational programs 91–2, 103
emotional abuse 86
exaltancy 75, 96
experiential leaps of faith 88–9

failure to learn from punishment
theory 8–10; and violent
coaching 102
family violence 91–3
fear 29, 32, 40, 51
first-hand knowledge 20

general prevention 97–8
grievous violent acts 4–5

haranguing 52–3; illustration of
53–4
heinous violent crimes 3–5, 64,
79, 97–8
holistic approach 15
humiliation 29, 41, 51 see also
self-deprecation

impotence see powerlessness
incessant melodrama 52
in-depth interviews 23
insoluble paradox 13
invidious comparison 50
intervention 91–7; during
belligerency stage 93; during
brutalization stage 91–3;
differential opportunity for
91; prime time for 94, 99;
and privacy issue 92; and
schools 94–5; during violent
performance stage 93–5;
after virulency stage 96–7;
during virulency stage 95–6